15-minute focus
Brief Counseling
Techniques that Work

REGULATION AND CO-REGULATION

ACCESSIBLE NEUROSCIENCE AND CONNECTION STRATEGIES THAT BRING CALM INTO THE CLASSROOM

NATIONAL CENTER for
YOUTH ISSUES

NCYI titles may be purchased in bulk at special discounts for educational, business, fundraising, or promotional use. For more information, please email sales@ncyi.org.

Duplication and Copyright

No part of this publication may be reproduced, stored in a retrieval system, or transmitted in any form by any means, electronic, mechanical, photocopy, video or audio recording, or otherwise without prior written permission from the publisher, except for all worksheets and activities which may be reproduced for a specific group or class. Reproduction for an entire school or school district is prohibited.

NATIONAL CENTER for
YOUTH ISSUES

P.O. Box 22185
Chattanooga, TN 37422-2185
423.899.5714 • 866.318.6294
fax: 423.899.4547 • www.ncyi.org

ISBN: 9781953945792
E-book ISBN: 9781953945808
Library of Congress Control Number: 2023903697
© 2023 National Center for Youth Issues, Chattanooga, TN
All rights reserved.
Written by: Ginger Healy
Published by National Center for Youth Issues
Printed in the U.S.A. • March 2023

Contents

15-MINUTE FOCUS
Regulation and Co-Regulation: Accessible Neuroscience and
Connection Strategies that Bring Calm into the Classroom

3

See page 106 for information about Downloadable Resources.

4

15-MINUTE FOCUS
Regulation and Co-Regulation: Accessible Neuroscience and
Connection Strategies that Bring Calm into the Classroom

Introduction

Have you ever seen a child break down at school—running out of the room, crying, throwing things, or refusing to do an assignment? It happens! I was that kid sometimes, and I bet you were, too.

One day in first grade, my teacher held a race around the school, and I was determined to win. I told my friends all morning that I would take first place. We gathered outside and lined up, and my teacher shouted, "Go!" but I didn't hear him. All the other students took off while I stood in disbelief, my feet stuck to the concrete. My teacher yelled, "What are you doing? Go, go, go! You are going to be last!"

Not only did I lose the race, but I also felt like I lost my dignity. Dysregulated, I started crying, then felt mortified when I couldn't stop while my peers laughed at me. At that exact moment, a lunchroom staff member saw me crying. She took my hand and walked me to the warm kitchen. It smelled so good. She pulled out a coloring book and crayons, sat us at a back table, and colored with me quietly.

"Okay, time to go back to class," she said when we had finished coloring a page together. I made it back in time for our weekly spelling test, which I aced. I am sure I wouldn't have done as well if she hadn't come to my rescue.

There were probably many other times before and after that experience when I was being co-regulated and didn't know it. I certainly didn't know it the day I colored with that kind woman working in the cafeteria, and maybe she didn't either. She wasn't a teacher or a part of the administrative staff, but she knew I needed to calm down before returning to class. She was a caring adult who made time for me, met me where I was emotionally, and guided me back to calm so I could do my best.

There is a link between student stress (which is what I experienced that day) and academic performance. Students struggle with attention, focus, and assignment completion when stressed. Alternatively, students perform better academically when their stress levels are tolerable. We can't erase all stress, and not all stress is bad. However, we want to help buffer student stress so that the stress level is manageable. Stress and the feelings that surround it are contagious! You've seen it before, right? An entire classroom, lunchroom, or gym in complete chaos from a negative emotional contagion. We can fix these situations. Let me rephrase that.

15-MINUTE FOCUS
Regulation and Co-Regulation: Accessible Neuroscience and
Connection Strategies that Bring Calm into the Classroom

5

We can *heal* them.

How do we do this? Safe relationships and positive connections. Academic success is more likely to be achieved when students feel safe, are connected to a trusted adult, and are emotionally regulated.

This book will teach you how to understand and work with the neurobiology of students and couple this knowledge with repeated compassionate responses. Together, this can positively change individual students and the whole school environment.

What Is Regulation, and Why Is It Important?

Regulation, or emotional regulation, is the ability to modify emotions and respond to situations with balance, calm, and control. Picture an alert, steady person who laughs, smiles, and is relaxed. These are signs that a person is effectively regulating. It's important to note that everyone is different, and regulation looks different for every student.

One of my favorite stories about different regulation presentations involves my son, Alec, who has the superpower of autism. In one of our family pictures, he stares into the camera with what many would describe as a grumpy face. This happens to be Alec's favorite picture. Every time he sees it, he says, "That was one of the best days of my life!"

Alec isn't thinking about the expression on his face; he remembers a gift he received earlier that day. It's important to know that we can't always tell a person's feelings by what their facial expression is or isn't showing. Alec appeared dysregulated but was quite regulated. Regulation is an individualized presentation on the outside and the inside. Learning what it looks like and feels like for ourselves and our students moves us closer to healing individually and collectively.

Dysregulation happens when an individual doesn't feel safe. Dysregulation happens when an individual doesn't feel safe. Their ability to function is compromised, and they cannot meet the demands of the external environment. Imagine a clenched jaw, forced smile, expression of anger, fast and impulsive movements, aggression, closed or squinted eyes, a tense body, and crying. These obvious symptoms and

15-MINUTE FOCUS
Regulation and Co-Regulation: Accessible Neuroscience and
Connection Strategies that Bring Calm into the Classroom

behaviors can be easy to spot, but what about the more subtle signs of dysregulation? Someone with glazed eyes and a blank face who is silent or speaking flatly. Someone who moves very slowly, slouches, and lacks curiosity. These are also signs of dysregulation.[1]

Both children and adults experience dysregulation every day, sometimes more than once. Knowing this provides many opportunities to practice and master healthy self-regulation and co-regulation. Co-regulation looks like warm and responsive interactions between two people (two adults, an adult and a child, or two children). The key to these interactions is that one person is attuned and perceived as safe, which soothes the other.

Humans are born to connect. We come into this world vulnerable, needing care, and not meant to be alone. Sadly, not every child receives ongoing safe, stable connections and attachments. And when those don't happen at home, we have to stand in the gap. It only takes one safe, committed, stable adult to help a child heal and build resilience through co-regulation.

Neurodivergence and Learning Differences

As we learn more about regulation, I want to be mindful of neurodivergent students. Neurodivergent means someone's brain learns or processes information differently than what is considered "typical." This term includes Autism, Dyslexia, Dyscalculia, Epilepsy, Hyperlexia, Dyspraxia, ADHD, Obsessive-Compulsive Disorder, and Tourette syndrome.

Research shows neurodivergent individuals often have difficulty regulating their emotions, which can lead to problems with anxiety, depression, and impulsivity. It is essential for those who are neurodivergent to learn self-care and self-regulation techniques to manage their mental and physical health.[2] No student can do this alone, and some students need more co-regulation than others, which requires intuition and commitment on the part of the adults around them. Being aware of student strengths, personal views, social and ethnic background, gender, and orientation and making considerations related to how their brains work is a critical part of ensuring self-regulation is a part of the skills they learn.

15-MINUTE FOCUS
Regulation and Co-Regulation: Accessible Neuroscience and
Connection Strategies that Bring Calm into the Classroom

7

Occupational therapist Kelly Mahler suggests significant shifts educators can make in their perspectives and practices to provide compassionate and practical support to neurodivergent students.

1. **Become trauma-informed**. Consider the trauma experienced by neurodivergent students who live in a sometimes overwhelming world that can feel unsafe.

2. **Move to a regulation-driven teaching model**. Compliance-based models condition students to please for reinforcers rather than listen to their bodies. Regulation-driven models help students feel safe and regulated in their bodies and environments through co-regulation.

3. **Provide a sensory-safe environment**. Some students are extra-sensitive to sights, sounds, smells, and other input that impacts the senses. Noise-canceling headphones, flexible seating, weighted blankets, and dampening lights can help students who feel overwhelmed in sensory-rich environments.

4. **Implement Interoception-based supports**. Yoga, Mindfulness, Meditation, and Breathing exercises can help students process what they feel inside their bodies and, in turn, help them manage and regulate their feelings.[3]

5. **Avoid Labels.** Labels influence expectations. Does a student's atypical behavior need to be changed? We can answer that only if we understand what function a specific behavior serves for them. Behaviors in neurodivergent students (repetitive behaviors, hand-flapping, vocal tics, rocking, pen clicking, being inflexible with change, seeking sensory input) can help them manage their surroundings in a world where they may feel they don't belong. Once we appreciate a behavior's adaptive function, we can decide if and how to intervene, hopefully increasing autonomy and regulation. Differences aren't deficits.[4]

One of my all-time favorite quotes is Temple Grandin's, "Different, not less." When we take differences off a diagnostic checklist and see them as adaptations to process information, we may see many behaviors such as "stimming," averted gaze, and ritualistic routines as ways a child helps themselves feel more comfortable in the classroom. We can view behaviors

15-MINUTE FOCUS
Regulation and Co-Regulation: Accessible Neuroscience and
Connection Strategies that Bring Calm into the Classroom

as personal accommodations. We would never consider taking away a child's wheelchair, right?

...traditional IQ tests often underestimate intelligence in the special-needs population.

Lastly, we should never assume a child's test scores accurately reflect intellectual functioning in neurodiverse populations. Most testing was designed for neurotypical children with neurotypical motor functions, meaning traditional IQ tests often underestimate intelligence in the special-needs population.[5]

One Size Fits One

This phrase, coined by Dr. Melissa Sadin,[6] is a paradigm shift from most parenting and educational approaches that look at the behavior, not the child. Most responses to behaviors are focused on reasoning, requesting, or offering incentives, rewards, or consequences. These approaches are reactive and flawed. They provide a one-size-fits-all answer based on a generic version of children and assume a child is intentionally behaving a certain way, or if they try hard enough, they can gain control of themselves. Unfortunately, these generalized approaches fail to account for a child's unique needs and traits at any given moment.

The paradigm must shift to account for the behavior trying to communicate a delayed need or skill. No matter the behavior, there is more than meets the eye.[7] We must take an individualized approach to truly meet a child's needs and respond in a way that will calm their nervous system and change their behavior. One size fits one.

One size fits one.

There isn't a checklist for helping students feel emotionally safe and connected at school. There isn't a checklist for what makes all adults feel safe and connected, either. But there are best practices that can and should be tailored to each educator and each student. We shouldn't pressure children to conform to what we consider "normal" when their nervous system prompts them to do otherwise. Differences are not deficits, and co-regulation is never the wrong answer.

15-MINUTE FOCUS
Regulation and Co-Regulation: Accessible Neuroscience and Connection Strategies that Bring Calm into the Classroom

9

This book holds unapologetic hope for healing and is laced with not-so-subtle guidelines to help relationships come first. Bruce Perry, renowned psychiatrist, educational researcher, and author, says, "Relationships are the agents of change, and the most powerful therapy is human love."[8]

Thank you for making space for this content. I can't wait for you to experience positive changes in your classroom. As you implement strategies and embrace this new lens of thinking and responding, there will be a domino effect. Everyone in your life (including you) will benefit from co-regulation!

As we start, it's helpful to be on the same page about the different facets of regulation and neuroplasticity. Here is a list of terms that we'll be using throughout the book:

Glossary of Key Terms

Adrenaline: A hormone produced in the adrenal glands released into the body as a stress response. It prepares the body to take action for fight or flight.[9]

Amygdala: Regulates fear and alerts us to danger, keeps us safe, aware of our surroundings, and away from potential harm. The amygdala can send false alarms and can become faulty when it is overactivated.[10]

Attachment: Lasting psychological and emotional connectedness between human beings. [11]

Attunement: Being able to tune in to a child's emotional safety. Allowing them to feel seen, known, and understood emotionally. Providing nurture proactively rather than making the child earn it.[12]

Blocked Care: When an adult becomes emotionally unavailable because their repeated attempts to care for and support a child are rejected. When a teacher tries to comfort or connect with a student in the classroom, they might get a range of push-away behaviors. Being continuously rejected, no matter your approach, is exhausting and deflating, and your adult brain may react with Blocked Care. It is often referred to as compassion fatigue.[13]

10

15-MINUTE FOCUS
Regulation and Co-Regulation: Accessible Neuroscience and
Connection Strategies that Bring Calm into the Classroom

Blocked Trust: When a child does not feel good enough about themselves to allow a safe connection.[14]

Co-Regulation: Warm, responsive, soothing interactions between two people (both adults and children). Attuned, communicative, and reciprocal exchanges.[15]

Cortisol: A stress hormone released during stress to alert the brain and body of a potential threat. High levels of Cortisol can cause brain fog, diminished memory, sleep deprivation, and dehydration, resulting in larger doses flooding the nervous system and creating more damage.[16]

Discipline: A response to behavior focused on strategies where students learn and grow from the experience. Not the same as punishment.[17]

Dopamine: The "reward chemical." Provides a sense of motivation to continue pursuing a given reward or need. Requires reactivation once the need or reward has been achieved. A dopamine deficiency is linked to depression, fatigue, apathy, and boredom.[18]

Dysregulation: When an individual's ability to manage and tolerate overwhelming emotions is compromised because the brain's cognitive state and body's emotional state are out of sync due to a real or perceived threat. Also called Emotional Dysregulation.[19]

Endorphins: A pain-relieving hormone that lessens the prediction of pain, reduces stress, triggers euphoria, and stimulates the immune system.[20]

Executive Functioning: Cognitive skills that allow us to focus our attention, plan and prioritize, be self-aware, have flexible thinking, and use memory recall.[21]

Fawn: A response to trauma presenting as appeasement, approval seeking, offering help, attention (connection) seeking, validation seeking, and letting others dictate behavior.[22]

Felt Safety: A subjective experience in which the brain and nervous systems feel genuinely safe and allow the child to relax and feel comfortable in a given environment. Just because the child is physically safe does not mean they truly feel safe.[23]

15-MINUTE FOCUS
Regulation and Co-Regulation: Accessible Neuroscience and
Connection Strategies that Bring Calm into the Classroom

11

Fight: A response to a trauma that presents as arguing, swearing, aggression, violence, challenging of authority, etc.[24]

Flight: A response to trauma presenting as being distracted, hyperactivity, running, hiding, avoiding, and more.[25]

Freeze: A response to trauma that presents as an inability to finish tasks, lack of motivation, withdrawal, "deer in the headlights," inability to move or talk, daydreaming, etc.[26]

Hippocampus: Part of the brain responsible for processing emotional information, as well as creating, consolidating, and maintaining memory. When the amygdala is activated, signals are sent to the hippocampus disrupting its ability to form memories. This part of the brain is critical for academic skills like memorization of facts and spatial memory.[27]

Mirror Neurons: Neurons in the brain that reflect the behavior of others (i.e., the brain perceives emotions another person displays and mimics them).[28]

Neurodivergent: A term used to describe someone with brain differences, such as Autism Spectrum Disorder (ASD), Attention Deficit Hyperactivity Disorder (ADHD), Obsessive Compulsive Disorder (OCD), Tourette's Syndrome, Epilepsy, and Dyslexia.[29]

Neuroplasticity: How the physical architecture of the brain adapts to new experiences and information, reorganizes itself, and creates new neural pathways based on what a person sees, hears, touches, thinks, practices, etc. Anything we give attention to or emphasize in our interactions creates new links in the brain. Where attention goes, neurons fire, and where neurons fire, they wire or join.[30]

Neurotypical: A term used to describe someone with typical neurological functioning or development.[31]

Object Constancy/Object Permanence: The understanding that items and people still exist even when you can't see or hear them. A blanket with a familiar smell, a picture, a plush, etc., can be used as tools for a child to keep/take with them to reinforce permanency and safety in a relationship when the adult is not near.[32]

12

15-MINUTE FOCUS
Regulation and Co-Regulation: Accessible Neuroscience and
Connection Strategies that Bring Calm into the Classroom

Oxytocin: The "love hormone" released through physical touch, proximity, or thinking about someone with whom we have an attachment, including pets.[33]

Prefrontal Cortex: The part of the brain central to emotional regulation, reflective functioning, and executive functioning, including judgment and mood.[34] The lower regions of the prefrontal cortex are instrumental in the regulation of emotions emerging from the limbic system.[35]

Punishment: A negative response to behavior focused on a consequence that may deter repeated behavior and inflict suffering. Not the same as discipline. [36]

Regulation: Skills used to calm physiological stress response systems, promoting emotional and behavioral flexibility through self-soothing. We are in this state when we can effectively manage, identify, and respond to our feelings and return to a balanced, calm state. Also called Emotional Regulation.[37]

Resilience: The developed ability to adapt to hardship and move forward.[38]

Restorative Practices: An innovative, trauma-informed approach to discipline and student accountability that moves away from punitive measures and focuses on healing, accountability, and change. Strategies in this field include community conferences, restorative circles, and victim/offender dialogues in both community and school settings.[39]

Rupture and Repair: The concept that healthy development depends on making mistakes and then offering the appropriate apology and repairing the situation.[40]

Scaffolding: Giving just enough support to allow children to learn skills independently, which helps them gain confidence in themselves yet recognize the benefits of support.[41]

Serotonin: A mood stabilizing, "feel good" hormone contributing to mood regulation and happiness. Influences sleep cycles and digestion.[42]

Stress: The neurological and physiological shift when someone encounters a stressor (threat). Not all stress is negative, but all stress causes a change within the body.[43]

15-MINUTE FOCUS
Regulation and Co-Regulation: Accessible Neuroscience and
Connection Strategies that Bring Calm into the Classroom

13

Stressors: Events that activate a person's stress response; can be external or internal circumstances.[44]

Toxic Stress: Chronic, excessive stress which exceeds a person's ability to cope, especially in the absence of supportive caregiving from adults.[45]

Trauma: A psychologically distressing event or pattern of events outside the range of everyday human experience. Impairs the proper functioning of the person's stress-response system, making it more reactive or sensitive and often involving intense fear, terror, and helplessness. Trauma isn't what happened to you but what happens inside of you as a response to what happened to you. The same event can happen to two people, but they may not experience it the same.[46]

Trigger: A sensory/visceral stimulus or set of stimuli that evoke the memory of a stressful/traumatic condition, emotionally and physiologically returning the individual to the place or time of the initial trauma (whereas stressors cause an immediate state of stress, strain, or tension).[47] Also defined as anything that creates an unwanted feeling, which can be external or internal but is different for everyone.[48]

14

15-MINUTE FOCUS
Regulation and Co-Regulation: Accessible Neuroscience and
Connection Strategies that Bring Calm into the Classroom

1

The Neuroscience of Regulation

Regulation 101

Regulation is the ability to alter, diffuse, or control emotions, also called self-regulation or emotional regulation. We regulate to self-soothe or calm down when our stress response systems are activated. It's about modification, not elimination, and finding balance when our emotions are off-kilter.

When regulated, we can better hear what others are saying, experience facial and vocal interchange, and mirror each other's tone of voice, volume, and facial expression. We are *with* one another. We are *in sync* and *attuned* to one another.[49] It's beautiful to move fluidly between challenges and success while accepting and managing the complex feelings that often accompany stress.

In terms of academics, a student who is regulated can:

- Learn
- Empathize
- Reason
- Be self-aware
- Solve problems

Regulation can feel like a clear head, lack of pain, and inner peace. Some describe it as "being in the zone." These skills are imperative to success in all areas of life.

I use the word "calm" a lot when I discuss regulation. It's essential, however, to point out that we shouldn't mistake emotional regulation for rejecting or suppressing emotions. Our overall goal isn't to be calm all the

15-MINUTE FOCUS
Regulation and Co-Regulation: Accessible Neuroscience and
Connection Strategies that Bring Calm into the Classroom

15

time! Why? Because not only is that an unattainable goal, but it also does not honor feelings like grief, loss, sadness, anger, and frustration. Though seen as "negative," these emotions are essential for growth. We cannot and should not shield any human from these feelings. Instead, we must learn to work through them, knowing we'll face challenges and trials. All emotions are normal, acceptable, and useful. We can help children learn this by expressing empathy and being with them through the ups and downs of all their emotions.

This leads me to co-regulation. Before the ability to self-regulate develops, humans need to experience co-regulation numerous times. Just like any other skill, emotional regulation has to be modeled and taught, and that is what we are doing when, as adults, we co-regulate with children. We don't heal in isolation. Children need safe adults, and students need teachers.

The need for co-regulation never ends, even when we are good at self-regulating. It's the best way to manage maladaptive coping behaviors when we are in a state of defense, also known as dysregulation. When a child detects a threat or senses danger, whether real or perceived, the warning system in their midbrain region (amygdala) alerts them that they are unsafe and need to do something about it. The child decides whether to fight the threat (fight response), run from the danger (flight response), play dead (freeze response), or appease and befriend the possible harm (fawn response) to protect themselves and survive.

The trigger for dysregulated responses can be as simple as a teacher announcing a pop quiz, to which a student may yell profanity because they feel unprepared. It can look like a child hiding in the bathroom because they fear danger during a safety drill. It can look like a student staring out the window, not finishing their assignment, because they miss the connection with their teacher out on maternity leave. It can also look like a student flattering a peer in hopes the peer will share answers on a test because their test anxiety feels unbearable.

The possibilities for how dysregulation is triggered and manifests in the school environment are endless. We don't always know what sets off the alarm in a student (another way of saying "what triggered the child" or "what activated their autonomic nervous system), and students may not be able to tell us. More important than identifying the trigger, adults must understand that the only goal for a dysregulated child is survival. Their autonomic nervous system disperses adrenaline and cortisol for

16

15-MINUTE FOCUS
Regulation and Co-Regulation: Accessible Neuroscience and
Connection Strategies that Bring Calm into the Classroom

this purpose. When this happens, the child needs help but may also resist adult intervention.[50]

I mentioned earlier that a regulated child could learn and solve problems. In the inverse, a dysregulated child is unable to learn and problem-solve. So, what does dysregulation look like in a school environment? You might see:

- Sensory and motor challenges (balance issues on the playground, avoidance of places like the lunchroom due to overwhelming sounds and smells)
- Processing delays (unable to understand or follow multi-step directions)
- Unusual pain responses (frequent school nurse visits)
- Hypervigilance (scanning classroom and hallways for threats)
- Difficulty communicating needs (missing assignments, failing grades)
- Lack of impulse control (can't sit still or wait in line)
- Over-compliance (raising hand obsessively, hanging out at teacher's desk)
- Lack of curiosity (staring out the window, saying "I don't know")
- Executive functioning delays (poor time management, disorganized, unable to plan and predict)
- Self-sabotaging behaviors (not handing in finished assignments, arguing)
- Problems with peer relationships (fighting, following, interfering)

What can and should be done when a child is dysregulated? So much! In the following pages, I will share basic neuroscience concepts to help shape your educator lens and lay the groundwork for recognizing patterns of stress responses demonstrating a need for regulation and co-regulation.

The graphic on the next page illustrates antidotes to stress hormones that can help heal us:

15-MINUTE FOCUS
Regulation and Co-Regulation: Accessible Neuroscience and
Connection Strategies that Bring Calm into the Classroom

17

D.O.S.E. Your Brain

DOPAMINE
"The Motivating One"
- Checking Off Lists
- Meditation
- Creative Activities
- Open to Learning/Curious

OXYTOCIN
"The Loving One"
- Safe Physical Touch
- Trust and Bonding

SEROTONIN
"The Calming One"
- Massage
- Cold Showers
- Walking in Nature
- Self-Acceptance

ENDORPHINS
"The Euphoric One"
- Exercise
- Laughing
- Dark Chocolate
- Physical and Emotional Pain Relief

Source: Attachment & Trauma Network, Inc. (2021).

ACEs and their Impact

ACE stands for Adverse Childhood Experience. This term describes the frequently occurring sources of stress children (from birth to 18) might suffer. In the original study, ten ACEs were researched and studied: physical, emotional, and sexual abuse, physical and emotional neglect, and household dysfunction in the form of mental illness, a mother treated violently, divorce, incarceration of a relative, and substance abuse. ACEs are categorized into Community, Household, and Environment. No matter how they are classified, the ACE study reveals the devastating effects of childhood trauma.

When bad things happen to a child while they are developing and growing, they are at greater risk for significant health problems and

18

15-MINUTE FOCUS
Regulation and Co-Regulation: Accessible Neuroscience and
Connection Strategies that Bring Calm into the Classroom

impairment in social, emotional, and cognitive development. ACEs are not a disorder or diagnosis but risk factors for long-term issues.

One in every four children in a classroom has experienced trauma and needs a safe adult who can co-regulate.[51] I would argue that this number is even higher after the collective trauma of the COVID-19 pandemic. School can be challenging for neurotypical children, but it is infinitely harder for kids who are more vulnerable due to diversity, neurodivergence, and high ACE scores.[52]

The higher a child's ACE score, the more likely they will have social and learning difficulties. In school settings, students who have experienced three or more ACEs have higher rates of academic failure, lower attendance, and more frequent behavioral problems. This book will encourage trauma-sensitive, trauma-informed, and trauma-responsive approaches with strategies to implement in the classroom and beyond.

A Little Neuroscience

Neuroscience research tells us that exposure to adverse childhood experiences, prenatal drug/alcohol exposure, or a mother experiencing significant distress during pregnancy can significantly sensitize the nervous system and impact brain development. These early exposures to ACEs directly influence a child's development and learning ability. Behaviors at home or school can be directly correlated to deficits from early adversities.[53]

Learning about brain development can offer a new perspective on responding to and working with children. Understanding developmental lags and how the brain is firing can shape adult expectations and responses to children's behaviors. A child's brain does not operate in isolation from the child's body.

The Brain Develops from the Bottom-Up and the Inside-Out

As humans, we come into this world vulnerable and dependent. We can't do many things yet because our brains aren't fully developed at birth.

15-MINUTE FOCUS
Regulation and Co-Regulation: Accessible Neuroscience and
Connection Strategies that Bring Calm into the Classroom

19

The brainstem and cerebellum are at the bottom of the brain, where survival functions like breathing, digestion, heartbeat, and blood flow are controlled. Our midbrain area, which houses our limbic system, develops next. The limbic system contains the amygdala and hippocampus, where our emotions are stored. The top of our brain, and the last to develop, is the prefrontal cortex, where executive functioning is housed.

And why do we need executive functioning? Education and academic success! With executive functioning skills, students can successfully listen, process what is said, and respond. Students can remember multi-step instructions while maintaining focus when their executive functioning skills work well.

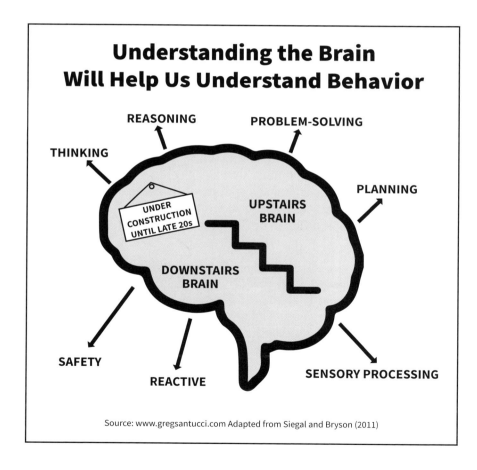

Understanding the Brain Will Help Us Understand Behavior

REASONING

PROBLEM-SOLVING

THINKING

UNDER CONSTRUCTION UNTIL LATE 20s

UPSTAIRS BRAIN

PLANNING

DOWNSTAIRS BRAIN

SAFETY

REACTIVE

SENSORY PROCESSING

Source: www.gregsantucci.com Adapted from Siegal and Bryson (2011)

20

15-MINUTE FOCUS
Regulation and Co-Regulation: Accessible Neuroscience and
Connection Strategies that Bring Calm into the Classroom

Why am I telling you this? Because if we are expecting a child to do things they haven't grown into yet or developed, we are setting them up for failure. Children and their brains must experience chronological developmental stages. If adverse experiences intrude upon a child's development, the child will struggle with social, emotional, cognitive, and physical development. Additionally, their executive functioning skills will be impaired. While they may appear physically capable of what adults ask them to do, they may not be developmentally capable.

Children who have survived traumatic events are often not their chronological age regarding their social, emotional, physical, and cognitive development. They may be developmentally delayed, meaning their brains haven't hit certain milestones or developed executive functioning, self-soothing, or self-regulating skills. When any child becomes dysregulated, they are acting from their midbrain and downstairs brain, and they can't meet the adult's requests until they are regulated.

Children cannot do more than their brains are ready to do. Asking a child to choose better behavior when they do not have a properly developing prefrontal cortex is like asking a child to fly.[54]

Use It or Lose It

The top part of the brain often referred to as the upstairs brain, is where the cortex and pre-frontal cortex are found. The brain is like a muscle in that what gets used develops, gets stronger, and performs better. When any area of the brain is ignored, it doesn't develop optimally, losing some of its power and ability to function.[55]

What wires and shapes our brain? Experiences—both good and bad. Children whose basic needs are not met as infants and young children do not learn to soothe themselves or trust that their needs will be met. They remain in survival mode, and their stress response system may be easily activated because unpredictability, lack of safety, mistrust, and chaos have been hardwired into their experiences. This stress response also results in a skewed worldview and self-view. They may believe they can only rely on themselves or are not good enough, among other things.

15-MINUTE FOCUS
Regulation and Co-Regulation: Accessible Neuroscience and
Connection Strategies that Bring Calm into the Classroom

21

An example of this could be a child who approaches everything from fear-based expectations because that is part of the brain that has been overused and has become strong. Or a child who flies off the handle at the slightest thing because the threat center of their brain has been overactivated. And what got pruned away? The ability to self-soothe and manage their feelings and behaviors. This is true for other parts of the body as well. If we go to the gym and only exercise our biceps, our leg muscles weaken and atrophy. Similarly, a child who has experienced neglect or abuse will have an under-developed and under-activated brain.

What Fires Together, Wires Together

Brains are computers with neurons and pathways like wires, made more robust and faster through repetition. Brains also want to be efficient and love patterns. When neurons fire together, they grow new connections. Over time, these connections can lead to "rewiring" in the brain.[56]

Think about what gets hard-wired in our brains. Driving a car is a good example. When we first learn to drive, we think about every little step and repeat it until we get it right. We look at maps, test the brakes, and remind ourselves to activate turn signals and wipers. We must learn and recall the rules of driving. But we don't think of each step after a few years of doing it consistently. Driving becomes automatic and seamless because our brains have created the "driving" neural pathway to the point of muscle memory. Sometimes we get to work without remembering how we got there.

Neural pathway wiring can be positive or negative. For instance, traumatized children may have hectic and disordered pathways due to circumstances. Chaos may be usual to them; some children even find it comfortable because it is what they know, are familiar with, and can control. This wiring helps explain these children's difficulties with events like transitioning into a new classroom or foster care placement. Even though the environment is safe, they do not feel safe, so they can't be calm or relaxed. They often feel uncomfortable and scared because their brain is wired to overuse their amygdala. Seemingly ordinary everyday events signal danger to their brain. When this happens, the child stays in survival mode continuously, resulting in constant fight, flight, freeze, and fawn behaviors.

15-MINUTE FOCUS
Regulation and Co-Regulation: Accessible Neuroscience and
Connection Strategies that Bring Calm into the Classroom

Neuroplasticity

Good news—brains can change. They are moldable!

It wasn't long ago that mental health professionals believed that our brains do not change once we reach adulthood. Scientists thought that after early adulthood, our brain structure and size were permanent. However, we now know neural connections are formed throughout life by experiences—especially novel ones—and when repeated, the connection between brain cells is strengthened and reinforced. Repeated trauma can reinforce the construction of the neural pathways leading to addiction and depression. Conversely, repeated positive experiences will reinforce pathways for self-regulated thoughts and actions.[57] Essentially, we can change brains!

Our job is to alter our mindset and shift our practices to reflect an understanding of how the brain and body function. Once we do that, we can help children build new and better neural pathways. We can also empower them to understand their brain-body connection by teaching them these neuroscience basics, which help them modulate their behavior, and gives them the power to heal themselves.

The following strategies work as individual or group activities when students are in their upstairs brains. Use the activities as a cognitive discussion/exploration with interaction and movement. During dysregulation, when students are operating in their downstairs brains and need co-regulation, you can reference these activities by reminding students of what they thought, felt, and learned when doing them. This will help shift the student's nervous system by knowing you "see" them and are with them in their dysregulation.

Strategies

Stormy Emotions: Sometimes, students don't feel they can survive overwhelming feelings. Emotions are like waves. They move up and down and get bigger during storms, but the storm will pass. Assure the student that feelings and emotions change and that how they are currently feeling or feeling during dysregulation isn't permanent. Validate their emotions. Encourage them to draw them out and express what they feel or have felt.

15-MINUTE FOCUS
Regulation and Co-Regulation: Accessible Neuroscience and
Connection Strategies that Bring Calm into the Classroom

23

Popping Problems: This activity can be used to practice breathing to calm overwhelming feelings surrounding a problem and give the child a sense of control. Chew gum and blow a bubble with the student. Help them picture one of their problems encapsulated by the bubble. The longer and more concentrated the breath, the larger the bubble. Explain this as creating more barriers and distance between the problem and the child. Once they blow a bubble, pop it, adding control and fun to the exercise. Explain that problems can be "popped" with perseverance and help. This activity also works as a distraction, helping to shift the child into play.

Let Your Worries Fly: This exercise gives control and action, which decreases cortisol and adrenaline. Have the child write their worries and fears on a piece of paper. Make a paper airplane and send it flying, metaphorically sending their worries away and letting them go. Explain that fears won't entirely disappear but can be managed by them as a pilot. Have them fly the airplane and explain that sometimes the plane will go straight, and sometimes it will go off course. Explain that planes also need a co-pilot, and together the child/pilot and the adult/co-pilot can guide the plane carrying worry and fear to where it needs to go. Explain that piloting takes a lot of practice and guidance; mistakes are essential to help us become better pilots.

Student Story

Principal Hill only knew a little about his new student, Jesse. Mr. Hill presumed Jesse had been through some struggles that could affect his academics and behavior, so he met with some of Jesse's teachers, who agreed to give Jesse preferential seating to help with focus and attention.

Within a few days, Jesse started arguing with other students in most of his classes. Mr. Hill began to meet with Jesse, hoping to establish trust. Jesse shared that he lived in an unstable situation and had a history of abuse. Mr. Hill also found out Jesse had experienced a traumatic incident when someone had hurt him from behind. Due to this, Jesse did not feel safe when other students sat behind him. Not being near the exit was also a trigger because it made him feel vulnerable. All of his teachers moved Jesse to a seat at the back of the room near the door. Now Jesse felt safer and more in control of his surroundings—which made a world of difference in his behavior.

24

15-MINUTE FOCUS
Regulation and Co-Regulation: Accessible Neuroscience and
Connection Strategies that Bring Calm into the Classroom

Remember: one size fits one!

Preferential seating is not a bad idea, but it depends on the student. Mr. Hill believes educators will never hurt students if they proceed as if they have been impacted by adversity. Trauma-informed strategies help everyone, and students with high ACE scores will significantly benefit from support and trauma-sensitive responses.

15-MINUTE FOCUS
Regulation and Co-Regulation: Accessible Neuroscience and
Connection Strategies that Bring Calm into the Classroom

25

QUESTIONS to CONSIDER

1. What behaviors have I noticed in the classroom that I may have misunderstood?

2. Do I have students experiencing high stress levels that can be better accommodated?

3. When a student is experiencing dysregulation, ask yourself, "What is in this student's way?" "What can I do to meet this child's need?"

4. At the beginning of the year and with a parent, ask the student:
   - What helps you feel better when you are overwhelmed, worried, frustrated, etc.?
   - What would help you be more successful at school?
   - (Check back throughout the year to determine if more strategies are needed. Also, evaluate what is or is not working.)

KEY POINTS

- Childhood adversity and student stress are common and will manifest in the classroom through behaviors. Childhood adversity can be healed through repeated positive interactions within safe relationships.

- Dysregulated children are not experiencing behavior issues; it's a brain thing. Understanding where the behavior is coming from (which part of the brain the child is operating from) should help determine your response.

- Recognizing and appreciating student differences and implementing approaches to individualized needs will help buffer stress for students.

26

15-MINUTE FOCUS
Regulation and Co-Regulation: Accessible Neuroscience and
Connection Strategies that Bring Calm into the Classroom

2 The Regulation Cycle

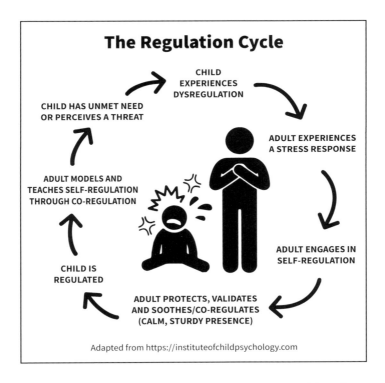

The Regulation Cycle

CHILD EXPERIENCES DYSREGULATION

CHILD HAS UNMET NEED OR PERCEIVES A THREAT

ADULT MODELS AND TEACHES SELF-REGULATION THROUGH CO-REGULATION

CHILD IS REGULATED

ADULT PROTECTS, VALIDATES AND SOOTHES/CO-REGULATES (CALM, STURDY PRESENCE)

ADULT ENGAGES IN SELF-REGULATION

ADULT EXPERIENCES A STRESS RESPONSE

Adapted from https://instituteofchildpsychology.com

As we examine this cycle, I want you to wear trauma-sensitive glasses. When working with a struggling child who needs you to co-regulate with them, ask yourself, "What happened to this child? What is this behavior telling me? What's the missing skill this child needs me to scaffold?"

If you go into a situation thinking, "I'm going to put a stop to this right now, no matter the cost," "They better respect me," "I will teach them a thing or two," or any variation of demanding control and respect, then do not engage in the situation. Acting on such thought processes can

15-MINUTE FOCUS
Regulation and Co-Regulation: Accessible Neuroscience and
Connection Strategies that Bring Calm into the Classroom

27

traumatize a child, ineffectively manage behavior, and damage the connection. We want to focus on the relationship to manage the feelings causing the behavior, not the other way around.

A Paradigm Shift

In my practice, a concept that helped me shift to understanding student behaviors and needs was the concept of the Iceberg.

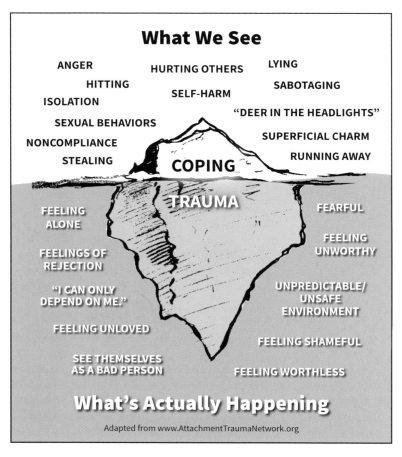

Adapted from www.AttachmentTraumaNetwork.org

Usually, the most frustrating behaviors we run into are when a child engages in purposeful, defiant, disrespectful, or manipulative actions. Some behaviors bother us when we feel we have worked on them tirelessly, but they don't stop. In those moments, I encourage adults to step back and get curious about what is happening.

28

15-MINUTE FOCUS
Regulation and Co-Regulation: Accessible Neuroscience and
Connection Strategies that Bring Calm into the Classroom

Think about an iceberg. The tip of the iceberg is visible, but most of the iceberg lies beneath the waterline. Think of the iceberg in terms of behavior and feelings. The tip of the iceberg may look like behaviors such as self-sabotage, lying, cheating, daydreaming, aggression, non-compliance, and superficial charm. However, these behaviors are coping behaviors for the feelings below the surface, like anger, pain, fear, self-loathing, shame, loneliness, and unworthiness resulting from unresolved adversity in childhood. These kids are often mislabeled as stubborn, dangerous, distracted, lazy, or attention-seeking when, in fact, they are connection-seeking, validation-seeking, scared, and unsafe.

Another concept important to the paradigm shift is *CAN'T, not WON'T*.

If a student senses any kind of danger or threat, the alarm system in their brain warns them that they need to protect themselves to survive. When this happens, a student **cannot** follow directions, hear what someone is saying, or even show "respect." They cannot meet expectations beyond survival. The skills they need to do things like be creative, find a solution, control their impulses, or delay gratification are in the prefrontal cortex, which is inaccessible during elevated stress.

The prefrontal cortex is the "lid" of the brain because it is on top. So, if a child has moved into a state of dysregulation, we can say they have "flipped their lid" and cannot use those skills located there. They are working from their midbrain, listening to the amygdala during dysregulation. We must get the lid back down so they can access it. We do this by helping them regulate. We need to shift them out of the midbrain and back into the upper part of the brain.

While a child may intentionally engage in the behaviors at the tip of the iceberg when they are dysregulated, this is not purposefully to cause harm or chaos. It's because they think the behavior will help their needs be met. This approach is usually all they know; it has been hard-wired into their brain. (Remember: What fires together, wires together). In these moments, it's not that the child **won't** do what you are asking; it's that they **can't**. Not yet. They can get there but may need you, a regulated adult, to help them.

15-MINUTE FOCUS
Regulation and Co-Regulation: Accessible Neuroscience and
Connection Strategies that Bring Calm into the Classroom

29

Step 1: Adult Regulation

Step 1 of the Regulation Cycle is about the adult, not the child. Regulation starts with the adult, who must be regulated before engaging in co-regulation and stay regulated during the co-regulation process. A dysregulated adult cannot regulate a child. In fact, a dysregulated adult can dysregulate not just one child but multiple children. But a regulated adult can regulate their entire classroom!

But it's not easy! One of the reasons it is difficult to keep cool while working with dysregulated children is that we all have specific "tripwires." We must identify and pay attention to these activators or triggers, as they differ for everyone. Behaviors such as lying, stealing, or manipulation can put one adult on the immediate defensive. In contrast, another adult can connect with the child and work through those same behaviors while remaining composed.

Think about what activates your ANS (Autonomic Nervous System) and what calms you down when triggered. In other words, what pushes your buttons, and what helps you handle situations when your buttons get pushed?

Triggers aren't always about behaviors in the classroom. Often, they are when we are physically tired, hungry, or depleted from giving. Our compassion for our students' big, negative feelings and behaviors can drain us. We can also have triggers from our history. Perhaps our triggers are things that bugged our parents, behaviors we got in trouble for doing, things we have never liked, or something we have experienced. No matter the source, we can implement solutions and prevention techniques once we identify our buttons.

Adult self-regulation prevention and maintenance tips:

Self-guided check-in: Ask yourself, "How am I doing?" and "How am I feeling?" Take a moment to notice what is happening inside you with honest introspection and vulnerability. When you sit with your symptoms and sensations, you may find discomfort you have ignored and avoided. Lean in, get uncomfortable, call it out, and address it. Otherwise, it can rear its ugly head in the wrong place, at the wrong time, and be displaced onto another person. If you check in with yourself and feel calm, cozy, creative, and able to problem-solve, then

15-MINUTE FOCUS
Regulation and Co-Regulation: Accessible Neuroscience and
Connection Strategies that Bring Calm into the Classroom

it's a good sign you are regulated and able to work with a child to further healing.

Awareness: Just knowing you are human and acknowledging certain things bug you calms your stress response. Leaning into uncomfortable thoughts or feelings takes their power away, puts you in control of your emotions, and lightens the sensitivity of trigger points.

Medical or Therapeutic Interventions: If you have an ACE score of four or more, you are at higher risk for long-term physical and emotional problems. Seek the help of a professional.

Active intervention tips when you become dysregulated while co-regulating with a child:[58]

Power in the pause: When you notice you are becoming dysregulated, pause. Identify what is happening inside you and decide what to do next. Doing so will slow your actions, making you more responsive and less reactive.

Take a physical break: Excuse yourself to use the restroom or get a drink. Grab a snack. Take a walk, and remember the power of pausing. Taking physical breaks can also reenergize and give your nervous system a chance to regain balance and meet a neglected need. It is also a great way to model regulation skills for children. It's a re-set that will open the door to co-regulation.

Take a mental break. Close your eyes and let your mind wander. Clear your thoughts, take a deep breath, and repeat a healing mantra. (See Resources)

Get perspective. Tell yourself what is happening is not personal, even though the situation may feel like it is. Behavior and disruption are not usually about you but a child's wiring and what happened to them. Focus on the relationship and what the child needs, not the behavior.

If you feel pressured by all of this, remember the goal isn't to be perfect. Watching an adult navigate moving back and forth between regulation and dysregulation is a potent learning tool for a student. Witnessing this takes the pressure off the student to be perfect.

15-MINUTE FOCUS
Regulation and Co-Regulation: Accessible Neuroscience and
Connection Strategies that Bring Calm into the Classroom

31

Self-regulation skills and co-regulation take practice. Staying regulated can be messy and challenging, but it is also the Regulation Cycle's first and most crucial step. The cycle can neither begin nor end unless the adult is emotionally regulated and able to re-regulate after dysregulation.

Step 2: Co-Regulation

This step is about supporting the student not only through listening but also support through physical presence. Our calm, warming presence can help calm a child's nervous system in a state of defense, even without words. Your tone, volume, and voice cadence are important when you co-regulate with a child. Don't yell. Stay calm. Speak quietly and slowly. Approach the child from the side or front, not from behind.

Gently ask the child to move with you to a safe and quiet place if they can. If they cannot move on their own or refuse, then meet the child where they are physically and emotionally by sitting or lying next to them. Little to no words are needed. Your physical presence can be enough. Your calm is an emotional contagion. Their chaos and dysregulation can also be contagious, so maintain confidence and gentle control. Go back to Step 1 as many times as you need.

Ways to support the child by "being with" and "doing with":

- Movement is the quickest and most efficient way to shift emotional states. Take the child on a short walk, do wall pushups together, or circle your arms. Whatever you do, do it together.
- Give them water and a protein snack.
- Pay attention to body language.
- Connect and be present in the moment. Put away any distractions.
- Listen, hold space, and allow feelings without judgment, no matter how irrational they seem.
- Empathize and validate. "I am so sorry this is so hard." "It makes total sense for you to be feeling this way."
- Avoid statements like "At least…" or "You shouldn't be upset about…" These statements minimize the child's struggle and might lead to further dysregulation.

32

15-MINUTE FOCUS
Regulation and Co-Regulation: Accessible Neuroscience and
Connection Strategies that Bring Calm into the Classroom

- Stay nearby. If safety is an issue, you can have a door or barrier between you.
- Offer regulation tools, such as:[59]
  - Breathing techniques: Blowing bubbles and pinwheels
  - Mindfulness exercises: Yoga and meditation
  - Fidgets and manipulatives: Try different textures
  - Sensory input: Weighted blankets or wrap, swinging, jumping
- Arts and crafts: Coloring, doodling, painting
- Journaling
- Bilateral movement: Tapping, jumping jacks, self-hug, music, or dance.

The overall goal is to make it clear that you "see" them and will be there no matter their behavior. Once the child is regulated and ready to talk, listen, and process, you can discuss what happened and what should be done next. It's essential to let the child know dysregulation will likely happen again. They need to know they are neither perfect nor are they expected to be so.

All the neuroscience from Chapter One can be shared with children in a simplified way. Teaching them to talk about where they are in their brain and how they feel in the moment is an essential step to regulating and regaining control. With practice, this grows more of the neurological loops needed to strengthen executive functioning and self-control. When children become dysregulated (especially in the classroom in front of other students), they often feel different and as if they don't belong. Normalizing dysregulation and teaching regulation skills can help relieve those feelings of shame or being different.

Step 3: Teach Self-Regulation

The development of self-regulation skills is dependent upon predictable, responsive, and supportive environments. The relationship between an adult and child is vital to self-regulation skill-building. Once a safe and predictable connection is established, we can teach regulation skills as a concurrent part of the co-regulation process.

15-MINUTE FOCUS
Regulation and Co-Regulation: Accessible Neuroscience and
Connection Strategies that Bring Calm into the Classroom

33

Modeling and teaching these skills have another benefit: they help you stay regulated. Seeing you regulate in front of them will have a stronger impact than just hearing about something they should try.

There are many ways to model and teach regulation; many different skills and tools can be woven into a daily school routine. Psychiatrist, author, and researcher Dr. Bruce Perry developed a model for using therapeutics in the education environment. Part of his framework centers around the six Rs that can guide teachers in implementing regulation strategies.[60]

- **Relational:** Tools and strategies should always focus on relationships and be connecting and co-regulating. Work with students, connect with them, learn about them, and be their partner in academics and healing.

- **Relevant:** Tools and strategies should be developmentally matched to the child and their emotional age rather than their chronological age. Students with adversities are often developmentally delayed, so interventions should be geared toward a younger age than the child's chronological age. Our expectations for a child should be flexible and relevant to them. Don't be afraid to implement techniques, games, tools, and strategies that seem younger in their focus.

- **Repetitive**: Tools and strategies should be patterned and repeated to promote predictability on the child's part. Implementing spiral learning will expand students' knowledge and improve their skill levels. Remember, "what fires together wires together" and "use it or lose it." The more you do something, the stronger it will become and the more ingrained it will be in the neural pathways.

- **Rewarding**: Tools and strategies should be fun and enjoyable. Follow the child's interests and preferences. Removing recess as a consequence should be avoided. Implement play and fun as much as possible.

- **Rhythmic**: Tools and strategies that are rhythmic and resonant with neural patterns are regulating and can be used proactively, as well as during dysregulation—singing, dancing, drumming, tapping, etc. Walking, swinging, and breathing are also rhythmic and regulating.

- **Respectful**: Tools and strategies always need to be considerate of the child, their family, and their culture. Belonging and inclusion

34

15-MINUTE FOCUS
Regulation and Co-Regulation: Accessible Neuroscience and
Connection Strategies that Bring Calm into the Classroom

create safety, leading the way to regulation. Never dismiss a child's experiences. Initiate conversations about culture and diversity.

Teaching self-regulation skills is not about teaching self-control. Self-control is halting unhealthy impulses which don't manage and heal the reason behind the behavior. When we are self-regulated, self-control is not as challenging. For example, if we get enough sleep, eat well, and feel balanced and steady, it's much easier to manage feelings when something upsets us. This is different from just managing behavior at the moment, which is self-control.

When a teacher actively and intentionally works to reduce stressors for children, it teaches children that everyone has stressors and there are things you can do to help yourself when you are in a stressful situation. Actively teaching self-regulation skills (especially keeping Perry's six Rs in mind) helps students identify their stressors and what works for them, reducing shame and behaviors that need consequences. We can't remove all stressors, but teaching students to use self-regulation skills and ask for co-regulation is vital so that they are able to meet challenges and build resilience.

Strategies

The following strategies work well to teach self-regulation through co-regulation and modeling so that when an adult is not present, the student can use them on themselves (This takes practice. Students should not be expected to self-regulate easily or quickly but can add tools as strategies to their toolbox through repeated practice and modeling.)

Give cold or hot drinks and snacks that allow chewing, crunching, and sucking. These can be helpful regulation tools because they can shift children out of stuck brain states through sensory input.

Voiced modeling is a process where you state your thoughts out loud, which is a powerful way to illuminate the thinking behind regulatory behaviors for students. "I need to focus before I start this next task, so I am going to take a few quiet breaths and then exhale slowly" connects the why with the how in real-time.[61]

Grounding is a form of distraction that helps the child (or adult) detach from emotional pain. Grounding does not solve the problem contributing

15-MINUTE FOCUS
Regulation and Co-Regulation: Accessible Neuroscience and
Connection Strategies that Bring Calm into the Classroom

35

to the overwhelming emotions but provides temporary support and works to prevent escalation. Grounding works well for children who often get stuck in the "freeze" response. Encourage students to plant their feet, sit on the floor, or press/lean against a wall. Pressure against a hard surface can physically ground them and bring them into the present. Have them notice and describe things they can see, hear, taste, hear, feel, and smell.

Self-hug can provide proprioceptive input, letting the child know where their body is in space. Ten-second hugs increase oxytocin, boost the immune system, ease depression, and lessen fatigue. Twenty-second hugs positively impact blood pressure and heart rate. Both send a message to the body saying, "I love you. You are okay."

Tap In/Tap Out is a system school staff can use to communicate with each other when help is needed. Set up a private Slack channel or other methods of communication for staff to request assistance. A team developed the following system at Mayflower Mill Elementary in Indiana to create a safe system of support:

- **Walk and Talk**: The student needs a safe adult to walk with them, co-regulate, and return them to class.
- **Hangout**: The student needs someone to sit with them in the classroom for a few minutes.
- **Flip-Flop**: The teacher needs someone to take over the lesson so the teacher can co-regulate with the student.
- **Delivery**: The student needs a safe escort to the office for a referral.

36

15-MINUTE FOCUS
Regulation and Co-Regulation: Accessible Neuroscience and
Connection Strategies that Bring Calm into the Classroom

- **Clear Room**: The student is aggressive or destructive. An emergency response by the support team to help transfer the rest of the students to another location is required.
- **S & R (Search and Rescue)**: The student has left the classroom without permission.

Help Is a Phone Call Away

If a student or staff member needs assistance, call _____

I Need a Walk and Talk in Room_____

Use this code if you have a student that has tried calming strategies in the classroom, but needs to do a lap around the school with an adult. The goal is for an adult to take the student on a brief walk to co-regulate, and then return them to class.

I Need a Hangout in Room_____

Use this code if student is in the room and needs someone to come sit with them for a few minutes. The student may be shutting down or in the "freeze" response. The goal is that someone will come and co-regulate with the child and the child stays in the classroom.

I Need a Flip-Flop in Room_____

Use this code if you want someone to take over your lesson, so that you can co-regulate with the student.

I Need a Delivery in Room_____

Use this code if you have a student that needs to be escorted to the office for a referral. Referring staff will need to complete an office referral form and send work that can be done independently.

I Need to Clear Room_____

Use this code if a student is being aggressive or destructive. This code triggers an emergency response by the TCIS Team and other staff to support potentially transitioning the class to another location.

I Need an S&R for _____ (Student Initials/Room Number)

Use this code if a student has left your area without permission. Follow with an office referral form and work to be completed independently.

Source: Mayflower Mill Elementary

15-MINUTE FOCUS
Regulation and Co-Regulation: Accessible Neuroscience and
Connection Strategies that Bring Calm into the Classroom

37

Student Story

As Miss Johnson was lining the students up for recess, she noticed Ben had removed his shoes and thrown them against the wall. She asked him to put on his shoes, and he refused. She made the request again with the same gentle tone of voice, and he replied with an even firmer "No." He was becoming more dysregulated by the second, and the other students were watching.

Miss Johnson took a deep breath, stayed calm, and dropped to Ben's eye level.

"Why don't you want to put on your shoes?"

He hung his head for a second.

"You can tell me," she said softer. "Are you worried about going out to recess and just want to stay inside?"

He looked her right in the eye and said, "No, Miss Johnson…my shoelace is broken."

Miss Johnson used the skills of connection and co-regulation even though she was exhausted and frustrated with Ben. And by using that connection, she got to the source of his objection. Because of her connection with Ben, he trusted her enough to tell her his problem. The other students witnessed the interaction, and feelings of safety likely increased for all of them. If she had expressed anger or disappointment and demanded compliance, the outcome would probably have been very different.

38

15-MINUTE FOCUS
Regulation and Co-Regulation: Accessible Neuroscience and
Connection Strategies that Bring Calm into the Classroom

QUESTIONS to CONSIDER

1. Who are the safe people I can call when I need to co-regulate or when I cannot co-regulate with a child?

2. Where can I go when I feel dysregulated?

3. What can I do to prevent acting out when I am triggered?

4. What part of the regulation cycle do I feel strongest in, and where do I need clarification and practice?

15-MINUTE FOCUS
Regulation and Co-Regulation: Accessible Neuroscience and
Connection Strategies that Bring Calm into the Classroom

39

- If you cannot remain calm during co-regulation, stop, do not pass go, and do not collect $200. Know that this is a normal response, and do not engage if you do not feel calm and capable. Don't despair. All is not lost. Try again; it will get easier.

- If your emotional or physical tank runs low, you are much more susceptible to becoming dysregulated.

- Co-regulation is modeling what we want to see—it is synchronicity. It's not a step-by-step checklist to follow. Every human is different, as are their needs. We must gently attune to a child's needs and lead them back to calm, peace, and safety.

- We can modify and reshape our school structures, such as environment, schedule, routine, academic and behavioral expectations, norms, and rules to better honor the biological needs of educators and the relational needs of the children in the classroom.[62]

- Regulation activities can be fun and keep the child engaged. Use laughter as much as possible, increasing felt safety and trust.

40

15-MINUTE FOCUS
Regulation and Co-Regulation: Accessible Neuroscience and
Connection Strategies that Bring Calm into the Classroom

Understanding Co-Regulation

What It Is, and What It Isn't

Relationships help regulate behavior. They go hand in hand.
Healthy relationships, this is how we heal.

– Nadine Burke Harris

Let's start with what co-regulation is—relationships!

Co-regulation is when a child and a nurturing, reliable caregiver share a sense of safety and engage in warm and responsive interactions to learn how to soothe and manage distressing emotions. The adult provides intentional modeling of the regulated state, and the child learns self-regulation. It helps the child understand their feelings, thoughts, and subsequent behavior.

Co-regulation is a dyad of attunement. Attunement is an intentional effort to connect and pay attention to what a child's verbal and non-verbal cues are telling us they need. When you meet that need, it gives the child a quick dose of felt safety. It's when the adult truly "sees" the child.

Co-regulation and trauma-informed responses are often misunderstood. I have heard many school counselors say they are accused of just playing with children or rewarding them for misbehavior. I spoke with a principal who regularly sits in his office with children building Lego towers and sharing snacks. He understands the traditional "time out" method or sending a student to ISS further dysregulates while "sticking close" and "being with" regulates. He receives many snide comments about letting students get away with behavior perceived as needing discipline or punishment. These commenters misunderstand the necessary skill and implementation of co-regulation in managing emotions and behaviors.

Let's break down what co-regulation is and isn't.[63]

15-MINUTE FOCUS
Regulation and Co-Regulation: Accessible Neuroscience and
Connection Strategies that Bring Calm into the Classroom

41

WHAT CO-REGULATION IS:	WHAT CO-REGULATION ISN'T:
Compassion During Struggle	Demands for Compliance
Relational Regulation	Behavior Focused
Modeling Emotional Management	Self-Implementation
Borrowing of Another's Calm	Grit
Compromise	Our Agenda
A Balance of Structure and Nurture	Imbalance of Structure and Nurture
Connecting with Curiosity	Assumption of Incompetence
Soft Tone of Voice	Sarcasm, Condescension, Judgment
Eye Level and Side-By-Side Intervention	Sending the Child Away/Time-Out
Emotionally/Physically Safe Environment	Unpredictability, Inconsistency
Accountability	Permissive
Boundaries	Free Reign
Discipline	Punitive

Co-Regulation is really about reciprocity. It's about social support. It happens through our non-verbal communication. It happens in my tone. It happens through my face. And through the tilt of my head. Showing that I care. That I'm listening. I don't have to solve the problem in that moment.

– Dr. Lori Desautels

Co-Regulation in the Classroom

A school can be positive and even therapeutic if the school's environmental structure is founded on boundaries, consistency, and

42

15-MINUTE FOCUS
Regulation and Co-Regulation: Accessible Neuroscience and
Connection Strategies that Bring Calm into the Classroom

predictability. There are rules, but more importantly, there are schedules and routines that students can learn to trust. Adults hold students accountable and walk them through that accountability. Still, those same adults also know that when students begin to dysregulate, they are communicating that their thinking brains are not online. Therefore, it is not the time for discipline but co-regulation. In this type of school environment, adults recognize they must wait until a student's brain is ready to hear, process, and collaborate before they can learn.

Children experiencing emotional or physical fear or pain cannot hear redirection, consequences, and instructions. In fact, the middle ear muscle expands with plasticity in "felt fear," so it can listen to all sounds in an environment. This adaptation for protection can look like hypervigilance or dissociation and is easily misjudged and consequenced. When a child is relaxed, these same muscles constrict for focus and attention. The ability to listen and process what is being said is located in that upstairs part of the brain, so if the child detects a threat, they cannot simply listen and follow directions just because they are being directed.[64]

Throughout the Regulation Cycle, it is important to hold space for the child emotionally. Allow the child to feel their feelings without judgment or "fixing" the problem. You can help the child understand that feelings can and should be felt rather than avoided. The adult doesn't work to eliminate feelings but instead allows the child to move through their feelings safely.

In doing this, you may need to tolerate unacceptable behavior or behavior that feels triggering temporarily. This sounds counterintuitive, but it is more effective to manage difficult behaviors because it helps decrease the need for them. Remember, the child seeks safety and survival, so the unwanted behaviors dissipate once felt safety is achieved.

If a student cannot process information and listen due to dysregulation, one of the best strategies to implement is **Reflection of Calm**. Use quiet, slow, and minimal words. Give positive affirmation to ground the child. "I'm here when you are ready," "You are safe," and "I am not leaving. ." This strategy is focused on being near the child. If the child doesn't want you near them, you can be across the room or on the other side of a door where they can hear you holding space and creating a sense of felt safety. Your calm regulation will be contagious.

15-MINUTE FOCUS
Regulation and Co-Regulation: Accessible Neuroscience and
Connection Strategies that Bring Calm into the Classroom

43

Co-regulation in the classroom can look like working individually with a child when they are dysregulated; it can also be modeled through group activities. For example:

- Music can be strategically used to settle or energize students.[65] Determine what the class needs:
  - Calming: 35-50 beats per minute
  - Focused work at desks: 55-70 beats per minute
  - Energize a tired class: 70-100 beats per minute
  - Fun and celebratory: 100-160 beats per minute

- Mindfulness exercises are great for regulating an entire group. Keep in mind safety and comfort come first. Always give the option to opt out of closed eyes, being fully quiet, bending, and floor positions. These may be triggering. For classroom mindfulness exercises, have students stay at their desks or have them all stand on their feet. Some activities can even be student-led, such as:
  - Breathing exercises
  - Large motor movement
  - Tighten and release
  - Coloring/arts/crafts

Accountability and Punishment

When dysregulation happens and a child requires intervention, we should never equate punishment with accountability. Punishment adds suffering to another human's life. There are ways to discipline without punishment but instead with consequences that instill accountability.

Let's look a little closer.[66]

Accountability is:

- Acknowledging you caused harm with your actions or behavior
- Understanding how others were affected by your actions
- Taking steps to repair the damage to those hurt

44

15-MINUTE FOCUS
Regulation and Co-Regulation: Accessible Neuroscience and
Connection Strategies that Bring Calm into the Classroom

- Giving back to the community
- Making a plan so it doesn't happen again

Punishment:

- Focuses on revenge and retribution for past perceived wrongdoing
- Teaches children to lie
- Rarely results in positive behavioral change
- Reinforces a failure identity
- Teaches what you don't want rather than what you want
- Sends the message when you don't do your best, people hurt you
- Teaches that making threats, taking things, and sending people away are valid ways to get what you want
- Models bullying

Predictable, consistent rules and collaborative consequences create safety and help manage behaviors. Consequences and building accountability work best when a child is involved in planning and deciding what happens next rather than imposing something on the child they may not understand. The concept of "rupture and repair" comes into play here.

Rupture and Repair

What is broken can be fixed.

Repairing a rupture and apologizing is one of the most powerful and restorative strategies a child can implement when they make a mistake. This is not only healing for the person they have hurt and for their relationship, but also for themselves.

When a child is ready to take responsibility for their actions, help them plan how to put right what needs to be repaired. This is individualized and depends on the child's age, developmental stage, and situation. A simple, sincere apology may suffice for one situation, but more complex and time-consuming reparation may be necessary for others. The critical piece needed for repair is the collaboration between the child and the person who was hurt—an adult should not solely dictate this.

15-MINUTE FOCUS
Regulation and Co-Regulation: Accessible Neuroscience and
Connection Strategies that Bring Calm into the Classroom

45

If a student has done something to an educator, the educator should actively offer an opportunity to start again, try again, forgive, and move on. One of the most effective ways to make apologies become second nature is to practice them when both the adult and child are regulated. In the middle of dysregulation, emotions are often too high to have the capacity to think outside the emotion and understand our role in the issue.

Engaging in restorative practices with a focus on healing and change is key. We must shift focus from changing behavior through forced apologies, lectures, and punitive consequences. When we allow the child to decide the outcome, this simultaneously gives more accountability and alleviates shame. Healing a ruptured relationship teaches the child a relationship can survive difficulties and helps children understand how their actions impact others.

This concept seems counterintuitive for some, but people heal by replacing punishment with attention, connection, and relationship. As a bonus, you will also see a dramatic reduction in behavior referrals.

A helpful concept to foster this collaboration with kids is "going back in time." Model this for kids when you say or do something you wish you hadn't done. Stop and tell the class to imagine traveling backward through time. Then reenact the situation by acting out what you should have done instead.

For example, one year, my children were fighting at a family reunion, and I was able to try it out. It went something like this:

Child 1: That's my cup. You can't have it! You are the worst!

Child 1 reaches over and yanks the cup, spilling the juice.

Child 2: I didn't know it was your stupid cup! Here, have it back!

Child 2 picks up the cup, ready to throw it at Child 1. Mom rushes over.

Mom: Everybody freeze! I know you both can do better. Let's jump in a time machine and start this moment over!

Mom walks backward, making a funny rewind sound. The kids laugh.

Mom: Okay. Let's start again.

46

15-MINUTE FOCUS
Regulation and Co-Regulation: Accessible Neuroscience and
Connection Strategies that Bring Calm into the Classroom

Child 1: Hey, that's my favorite cup. Can I use it?

Child 2: Sorry. It was the only clean one. I am almost done, and then I'll wash it for you.

To be honest, I was in awe of what happened. It worked so well. Shortly after, I pulled both boys aside and discussed their feelings, which were amplified because the whole family witnessed the event. This discussion helped them name those feelings of embarrassment leading to escalation, and then they were able to apologize. The apology worked because the tension was gone, the rupture addressed, and they could see the moment as a misunderstanding that could have been handled differently.

Now, let's think about times when adults cause a rupture in their relationship with a child. For example, an adult has yelled at a child. In this scenario, the adult needs to take a breath, return to step one in the Regulation Cycle, apologize, and try again.

Rupture & Repair

Rupture is inevitable. Repair takes work.

Repair is more than "I'm Sorry."

It's also:
- Acknowledging that it happened
- Owning our role
- Naming the impact (and listening to their version)
- Talking through how it was co-created
- Planning a path forward

Source: Lindsay Braman

Apologies from the adult to the child in these situations are critical. The apology models precisely what we are hoping the child will eventually be able to do on their own without prompting. If the adult doesn't apologize,

15-MINUTE FOCUS
Regulation and Co-Regulation: Accessible Neuroscience and
Connection Strategies that Bring Calm into the Classroom

47

the opportunity for healing is lost. Repairing the rupture provides "felt safety" for the child, strengthens the relationship, and builds resilience.

Building Resilience

The more experiences of co-regulation within positive relationships we have, the more resilient we become. Resilience is the adaptive ability to overcome hardship and spring forward. Resilience is grown, not inherent, and like co-regulation, resilience is not a solo act.

The most common factor for children who develop resilience is at least one stable and committed relationship with a supportive parent, caregiver, or another adult. A positive and safe relationship is the active ingredient in developing resilience. A committed adult can buffer a child from the full impact of a traumatic event and can keep the stress from becoming toxic.[67]

How do we build resilience?

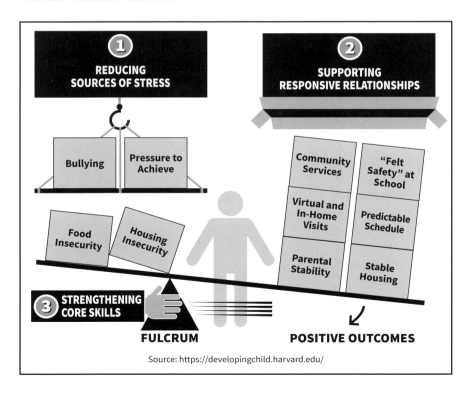

Source: https://developingchild.harvard.edu/

48

15-MINUTE FOCUS
Regulation and Co-Regulation: Accessible Neuroscience and
Connection Strategies that Bring Calm into the Classroom

- Remove negative experiences
- Increase positive experiences
- Strengthen child-adult relationships and support

For children to develop resilience, they must have resilient adults in their world who can pour love and attention into them. In other words, we must build resilience in adults and children.

Strategies

The first two strategies below help a child move forward emotionally after dysregulation. Both require a co-regulating partner and should be done only when students are in their upstairs brains and regulated. These strategies open the door to discussion and thought processes that can lead the student to proactively self-regulate in future moments after reviewing past moments of dysregulation.

The Dance of Attunement/Getting in Sync: Have a student put earbuds in with one type of music (fast and loud) and have another student put earbuds in with a different kind of music (slow and quiet). Have them try to dance together (no touching is necessary). Discuss attunement and being in sync. Tell them to draw or describe a time they felt in sync with someone, then draw or describe a time they felt out of sync in a relationship. Discuss how being out of sync can lead to miscommunication and misunderstanding. Explain that we need to hear each other's side and listen without judgment to fully understand another person's perspective before we jump to conclusions or say and do things in the heat of the moment.

Backward Chaining: Draw a chain link or use a real one for this activity. Start with the last link in the chain and name the previous event before an adult intervened (i.e., throwing a chair or skipping class). Have the student draw or touch the previous link and identify what happened before that. Repeat for each link until the student has reached the link (precipitating event), which set the whole "chain of events" in motion. It could be something like "I felt hungry," "I was jealous," or "My parent yelled at me." Identify what could have been done differently in the link after the precipitating event. Depending on the age and developmental stage of the student, they may need guidance in this. Avoid judgment as you bring awareness to where the chain could have stopped.

15-MINUTE FOCUS
Regulation and Co-Regulation: Accessible Neuroscience and
Connection Strategies that Bring Calm into the Classroom

49

Pulse Oximeter: The Neurosequential Model of Education by Dr. Bruce Perry teaches that regulation can be quantified through Pulse Oximeters. Students can document their heart rates before, during, and after stressful situations. Linking heart rate tracking with body awareness increases students' understanding of the power of regulation and allows students to understand what helps them regulate successfully. It gives them the ability to practice self-regulation as they watch their heart rate change through deep breathing, grounding, and talking with someone they trust.[68]

Pulse Oximeters can be used in a calm kit or regulation space.

Model and teach students the purpose of using the pulse oximeter first on an adult and then have them practice using it on themselves when calm to establish a baseline. Place the pulse oximeter on the child's index finger the entire time, and take long, slow, deep breaths. Have them watch their heart rate lower as they practice deep breathing.

You can also use the pulse oximeter with the following:
- Guided mindfulness meditations
- Muscle relaxation
- Watching a calming visual, like a glitter jar
- Stretching or a slow yoga sequence
- Lying flat on the floor and doing belly breathing

When a student becomes dysregulated, ask the student if they would like to try using the pulse oximeter to help them manage the feelings they are having. Place the pulse oximeter on the student's index finger and have them notice the numbers, then gain control of the numbers through breathing and other mindfulness strategies.

Popsicle: This activity can be done with the child during co-regulation or with all students as a preventative brain break. Have students tighten up all their muscles as hard as they can. Then have the students "melt" (like a popsicle) each part of their body slowly, starting by softening their feet, then ankles, then shins, etc. Challenge them to see how slowly they can "melt." This helps drain cortisol and adrenaline from the body while encouraging muscle awareness and relaxation.

50

15-MINUTE FOCUS
Regulation and Co-Regulation: Accessible Neuroscience and
Connection Strategies that Bring Calm into the Classroom

Student Story

Mr. Blevins, the high school counselor, and Miss Talbot, the principal, met and formulated a plan to help the school become more trauma-sensitive. They met with the staff at the beginning of the year and trained each person in the building to better respond to students by understanding which part of the brain students were operating from during dysregulation. They then went into every classroom and taught the students basic neuroscience and modeled different strategies to implement when the students felt dysregulated. The staff began to see profound results! The French teacher noticed that many students had test anxiety, so before every test, she used guided meditation with the students. Test scores rose, and students commented on how the meditation time helped lower their anxiety levels.

One day a student named Gabby came into Mr. Blevins's office after she flipped a desk because another student was making fun of her. Mr. Blevins asked Gabby if she felt ready to talk yet. She was not ready, so they sat together quietly until Gabby said, "Mr. Blevins, I think this is one of those times you talked about where I was in my downstairs brain. Before you call my mom, can you do some mindfulness with me?"

Gabby was able to ask for what she needed because Mr. Blevins instructed the class on regulation techniques when the students were in their upstairs brains and ready to learn, which is when explicit instruction works best.

15-MINUTE FOCUS
Regulation and Co-Regulation: Accessible Neuroscience and
Connection Strategies that Bring Calm into the Classroom

51

QUESTIONS to CONSIDER

1. When I make a mistake with a student, how can I repair that trust with them?

2. What can I do as a teacher to increase classroom safety, predictability, and trust?

3. In what specific ways can I increase positive experiences in the classroom for students who are struggling?

4. How can I personally help build resilience in my students?

KEY POINTS

- Actively teaching, giving feedback, practicing skills, and having discussions with students is always a good idea, but it cannot be done until the student is regulated and has access to their prefrontal cortex.

- Time the lesson when the student is ready to hear and process. If the student begins to dysregulate, then pause and focus on regulating the student. Sometimes tasks need to be given in small doses intermittently, not all at once. The effectiveness of any task depends on the student's level of regulation.

- Co-regulation is a philosophy, not a checklist. It requires a relationship and safe connection. Self-regulation skills take years to develop through the repetition of co-regulation because memory and processing are impaired during dysregulation. The need for co-regulation never ends.[69]

- Resilience is adapting and thriving after a crisis, not just surviving it.

52

15-MINUTE FOCUS
Regulation and Co-Regulation: Accessible Neuroscience and
Connection Strategies that Bring Calm into the Classroom

Bottom-Up vs. Top-Down Strategies and Implementation

4

What Do Bottom-Up and Top-Down Mean?

The brain develops from the bottom-up and inside-out.

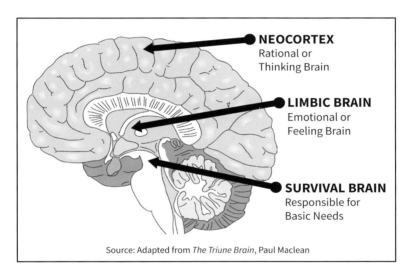

NEOCORTEX
Rational or
Thinking Brain

LIMBIC BRAIN
Emotional or
Feeling Brain

SURVIVAL BRAIN
Responsible for
Basic Needs

Source: Adapted from *The Triune Brain*, Paul Maclean

Bottom-Up refers to a sequential order in brain development and functioning. The first parts of the brain to grow are the brain stem and cerebellum. Located in the lower part of the brain, this is where heartbeat, digestion, breathing, and other functions we need for basic survival are located. This is why it is also called "the survival brain."

The next part of the brain to develop is the mid-brain, where the limbic system houses the threat detection system, and the amygdala is the alarm bell. The last part of the brain to form is the highest part of the brain, composed of the cortex and the pre-frontal cortex. In this part of the brain, we find functions such as planning, task initiation, working memory,

15-MINUTE FOCUS
Regulation and Co-Regulation: Accessible Neuroscience and
Connection Strategies that Bring Calm into the Classroom

53

personality expression, moderating social behavior, and controlling certain aspects of speech and language. Development of executive functioning continues through adolescence and early adulthood.

When we talk about students being in their survival or downstairs brain, we are talking about students only being able to access and use the parts of the brain responsible for survival and basic functions. As such, Bottom-Up strategies refer to tools that work for dysregulated and stuck students.

Top-Down, on the other hand, refers to the cortical or upstairs part of the brain. When we use Top-Down strategies, the child should be regulated and have access to all parts of their brain. If you use a Top-Down approach and the student does not have full access to their upper brain due to dysregulation, the strategy will not work and may harm the relationship.

These two categories have entirely different causes and therefore require other interventions. How do we know which parts of the brain are firing? We can look at behavior.

BOTTOM-UP BEHAVIORS	TOP-DOWN BEHAVIORS
Instinctual and Unintentional	Deliberate and Intentional
Survival-Based Stress Responses	Can Take Years to Develop
Controlled by the Lower Brain/ Limbic System	Requires a Connection to the Cortex
Infants Only Have Bottom-Up Behaviors	Requires Higher Developmental Age
Child Cannot Control	Child Can Control
Arise When the Child Senses Danger	Arise When Threat Is Not Apparent

When adults attempt to manage challenging (Bottom-Up) behaviors using point sheets, sticker charts, level systems, seclusion, or restraint, it doesn't work and can make things worse. These approaches are shame-based and assume all behaviors are deliberate and should be dealt with through punishments, consequences, or rewards. Bottom-Up behaviors do not respond to rewards, consequences, or punishments because they are brain-based stress responses that require understanding, compassion, and actively helping an individual feel safe based on their unique neurology.[70]

15-MINUTE FOCUS
Regulation and Co-Regulation: Accessible Neuroscience and
Connection Strategies that Bring Calm into the Classroom

When in doubt, use Bottom-Up interventions. Brain-based discipline strategies work for everyone, and helping students feel safe should always be the first approach. Only after we see a student become regulated should we attempt Top-Down methods that require the child to reflect, talk, and problem-solve.

Implement a Top-Down approach when:

- Breathing has returned to normal
- Eyes are focused
- Speech patterns and response times are quicker
- Student can control their body
- Student can respond calmly

It is crucial to focus on the relationship, not the behavior, and continue to work on connection, validation, and affirmation.

It's important to note even if the student appears ready for a Top-Down approach, they still may not be prepared to deal with consequences or accountability. It is crucial to focus on the relationship, not the behavior, and continue to work on connection, validation, and affirmation.

It is also essential to "connect before you correct," which is another way of saying Bottom-Up before Top-Down. Avoid telling the child what to do and be there for them and with them. Assume they would do better if they could. You can engage in discussion when the child is regulated. But the connection must come first. "I accept you. The behavior can change, but my acceptance of you won't change." This is about unconditionally supporting the child no matter what they throw at you. Send the message that you will still be there whether they are calm or dysregulated, at their best or worst.

Please avoid:

- Comparison statements
- Shaming statements such as, "You shouldn't feel that way," and "What is wrong with you?"
- Questions and statements the child cannot comply with, like, "Why are you doing that?" and "Stop."

15-MINUTE FOCUS
Regulation and Co-Regulation: Accessible Neuroscience and
Connection Strategies that Bring Calm into the Classroom

55

- Hijacking the space and conversation by talking about your experiences and dismissing theirs[71]

Bottom-Up Strategies

Movement is the fastest, most efficient way to relieve the body of stress hormones and shift from dysregulation to regulation.[72] Start with large movements, and as the student begins to regulate, modulate down to smaller and quicker movements. (Arm circles, marching, a walk outside, jumping, swinging, rocking, etc.). Movement also introduces calming chemicals into the child's body.[73]

Sensory-Connected Thought Bubbles can help with grounding. Prompt the student to notice something in the room. Have them write or draw what they notice in the thought bubble. Ask them to fill in as many details as possible about what they notice. This exercise is about awareness and bringing them back into regulation.

Body Scan is another grounding technique. Ask the child to notice and describe verbally or through drawing different parts of their body and the reaction that happens when they are experiencing a dysregulated feeling. Encourage them to examine what is going on inside their body when they worry. Use the following questions as prompts if they need help:

- What hurts?
- Do you notice a change in body temperature? Hot or cold?
- Do your eyes burn?
- Ringing in ears or difficulty hearing?
- Shakiness, pounding, or soreness?
- Difficulty breathing?
- Nausea or stomach pain?
- What else do you notice?

Have them scan their body and discuss possible sensations. A word list like the one following can be helpful when asking children about different body sensations. They can circle the words, make up their own, or draw what they are feeling.

56

15-MINUTE FOCUS
Regulation and Co-Regulation: Accessible Neuroscience and
Connection Strategies that Bring Calm into the Classroom

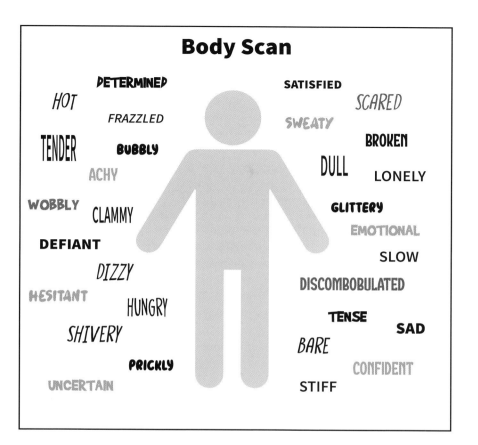

Body Scan

DETERMINED · HOT · FRAZZLED · SATISFIED · SCARED · SWEATY · TENDER · BUBBLY · BROKEN · ACHY · DULL · LONELY · WOBBLY · CLAMMY · GLITTERY · EMOTIONAL · DEFIANT · SLOW · DIZZY · DISCOMBOBULATED · HESITANT · HUNGRY · TENSE · SHIVERY · SAD · BARE · PRICKLY · CONFIDENT · UNCERTAIN · STIFF

Stress Awareness is a tool that decreases stress by bringing attention to feelings and sensations while gaining control through the act of noticing. Once the student is regulated, have them again rate their level of stress. Encourage the student to notice and share what happened between the first and second numbers.

Play reduces a child's stress and is more about the relationship than the specific game. The connection between an adult and a student grows when the environment is playful, safe, and fun. For Bottom-Up interventions, play something simple side-by-side. If the child is dysregulated, be the leader and let them join in. If the child is regulated, they can lead, and you can follow.

15-MINUTE FOCUS
Regulation and Co-Regulation: Accessible Neuroscience and
Connection Strategies that Bring Calm into the Classroom

57

Top-Down Strategies

Happy Memory/Calm Place is a mindfulness exercise. Prompt the student to think of a time when they felt safe, content, relaxed, and at peace. Then ask the student to imagine or tell you what they see, hear, feel, and think, describing their happy memory/calm place in detail. Encourage the child to write or draw this place, and remind them they can go there in their mind anytime they need comfort. During dysregulation, when they need a Bottom-Up strategy, you can prompt them to think of their Happy Memory/Calm Place. If you know the details, you can quietly and gently reflect those details to the student.

Positive, Negative, and Unrealistic Solutions is a problem-solving strategy. Prompt the student to describe a problem they are facing in one sentence. Then have them draw three empty thought bubbles, titling one "Unrealistic," one "Negative," and one "Positive." Have them write a solution to their problem in each bubble. This helps the child see the big picture and know they aren't locked into a reaction, takes the shame out of the problem, and gives them control. They can learn that they have choices and opportunities for any problem. Depending on their age and developmental level, they may need more or less guidance.

Emotional First Aid Plan is a proactive exercise to help children plan for when they are dysregulated. Have the child describe objects found inside a First Aid kit (e.g., bandages, splints, antibiotic cream, sterile wipes, gauze, etc.). Explain an emotional First-Aid plan can support and provide relief when they feel scared, angry, anxious, or sad. Draw a picture of a First Aid kit and have the child answer the following prompts to create their individual plan for when they are dysregulated:

- Safe place to go
- Safe person to talk to
- Favorite grounding tools
- Favorite breathing techniques
- Favorite affirmation

Journal Jar is a writing exercise. Fill a jar with journal prompts (See Resources). Tell the student they can "Name it to tame it" (decrease the power of their worries by calling them out rather than hiding them) through writing. This will also help them learn to listen and build trust within

58

15-MINUTE FOCUS
Regulation and Co-Regulation: Accessible Neuroscience and
Connection Strategies that Bring Calm into the Classroom

themselves, creating felt safety. This will reduce fear and anxiety, as well as strengthen and control their memories while creating new narratives.

This or That is a proactive, thought-provoking exercise. Ask the child, "When you get dysregulated, what do you immediately want to do? What is your gut reaction?" Have them speak, write, or draw their answer. Then have them answer, "What are some alternatives to try the next time you get dysregulated?" Have them compare the two and determine which is the better choice.

Student Story

I met two high schoolers on the verge of not graduating who taught me an important lesson. They both struggled academically and behaviorally and were about to be suspended for too many absences. I couldn't reconcile a plan where we were sending them away when they needed us most. Wasn't our goal to help them graduate? I knew we could do better and worked to build relationships with them. Everything changed when these two students felt safe enough to share their stories.

Brooklyn told me a teacher told her she would never amount to anything. She stopped coming because she saw no point in attending school if she was a failure. Why would she try to complete assignments or ask for help if she had no potential?

Austin shared that he overheard his new principal, Mr. Dawson, talking to several of his teachers after he transferred to a new school. Mr. Dawson told the other teachers stories a teacher at Austin's old school shared and told the teachers to keep their distance from Austin—for their safety. Austin walked out and didn't come back. Can you blame him? When working with students, we must set aside our biases and triggers. This is especially true when working with teens who have built up thicker walls and defense mechanisms. We can't give up, no matter how hard they try to push us away. We should be curious about students who won't answer our questions, especially when they are being "obstinate" or "disrespectful." **Students grow at the pace of trust.** Some relationships take longer to build because they fear trusting an adult who may hurt them when they are most vulnerable.

15-MINUTE FOCUS
Regulation and Co-Regulation: Accessible Neuroscience and
Connection Strategies that Bring Calm into the Classroom

59

1. How can I connect with students in a Bottom-Up way?

2. How can I connect with students in a Top-Down way?

3. How can students help each other with these interventions in the classroom?

KEY POINTS

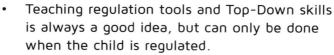

- Teaching regulation tools and Top-Down skills is always a good idea, but can only be done when the child is regulated.

- Awareness and grounding skills become stronger and easier with practice. The more they are used, the more quickly a child can make the connection that when they feel dysregulated, they can get back into a regulated state faster by implementing what they know works best for them.

- Bringing awareness to feelings helps students realize that emotions are there for a reason. They need to know there is a neurobiological reason for their behavior, which allows them to understand that they can name it, control it, and move through it.

- Recess and brain breaks with movement throughout the school day will help prevent and alleviate dysregulation.

60

15-MINUTE FOCUS
Regulation and Co-Regulation: Accessible Neuroscience and
Connection Strategies that Bring Calm into the Classroom

5 You Are the Strategy

I can recommend all the tools and strategies in the world for regulation, but the truth is the very best strategy is **you**. For some, this can feel like a heavy burden, and that's okay. This book is not meant to pressure anyone. If this is how you feel, sit in that awareness. Instead of diving right in before you are ready, you may need to explore your own nervous system (see Chapter 7).

Your nervous system matters! Our brains and bodies hold the state of our nervous systems, and it takes a regulated adult to regulate a student. It also takes a regulated nervous system to heal and move forward from a state of being stuck. You may not be ready to help others because you need help first. Find people who make you better, who believe in you, and who are your safe base. That's where you will find the growth and healing we all need.

You can be the caring adult who makes all the difference in the world for a child! Your everyday interactions with students carry power and you can be a messenger of safety, or a bringer of hope and healing. The graphic below shows that our regulation can lead to attachment when we are attuned to the child.

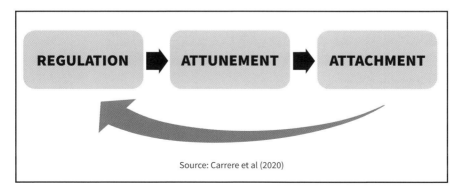

Source: Carrere et al (2020)

15-MINUTE FOCUS
Regulation and Co-Regulation: Accessible Neuroscience and
Connection Strategies that Bring Calm into the Classroom

61

Imagine if we measured success by the amount of safety that people felt in our presence.

– Jonathan Louis Dent

Mirror Neurons

Co-regulation is modeling what we want to see. What we reflect is reflected back to us via mirror neurons. Mirror neurons are nerve cells in the brain that activate when you perform an action and then witness someone perform the same action. This is different from other neurons that fire when you act alone.

As educators, our calm can be as contagious as the students' chaos. We can control the emotions in the room and let the student(s) know we will continue to be there for them no matter their behavior. They need to know relationships come first. Mirror neurons will help a student regulate if the adult is emotionally attuned and physically available. This is the difference between co-escalation and co-regulation.

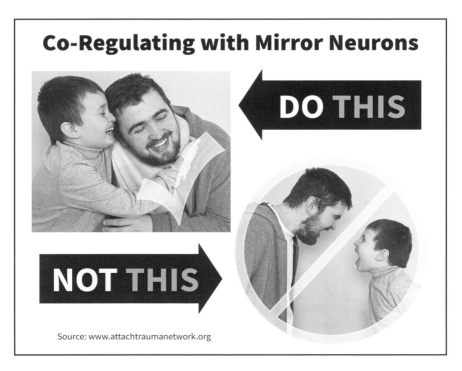

Source: www.attachtraumanetwork.org

62

15-MINUTE FOCUS
Regulation and Co-Regulation: Accessible Neuroscience and
Connection Strategies that Bring Calm into the Classroom

CO-ESCALATION	CO-REGULATION
Narrowed Eyes	Warm, Soft Gaze
Clenched Jaw	Relaxed Face
Tight Fists	Pause and Breathe
Standing Over	Kneeling Down
Lecturing	Fewer Words
Blaming	Avoiding Judgment
Shaming	Validating
Elevated Volume	Listening
Shallow Breathing	Deep Breathing
Quick Movements	Slowing Down[74]

If you are going to be the strategy, let it be through positive mirror neuron experiences in safe co-regulation. Wrap children in safety and connection. Firefighters run into burning buildings to put out fires, but teachers run into the building and create a relationship with that fire.

– Dr. Melissa Sadin

Source:@realnasty adapted @mamidientes posted by the Therapist Parent 2021

15-MINUTE FOCUS
Regulation and Co-Regulation: Accessible Neuroscience and
Connection Strategies that Bring Calm into the Classroom

63

You are the strategy. Don't underestimate your power.

The Power of One

*It's not rocket science; it's brain science. The heart of being a
trauma-responsive educator is to understand the power of one.*
– Jim Sporleder

Jim Sporleder was the principal of a school where students had
experienced an average of 5.5 ACEs. As you can imagine, with a student
body this dysregulated, the staff constantly put out fires and felt like
they were not making a difference. Under Jim's direction, they shifted
their focus to prevention through building relationships. By the time
he retired, 70% of students were functioning as if they had zero ACEs.
The trauma-responsive culture enveloping the school and the safe
relationships they had within the school helped the students thrive.
Both played an important role in their students looking toward the
future with optimism—they had built resilience. And remember that the
most common factor in building resilience in a child is a positive, safe
relationship with at least ONE stable, committed adult. It only takes ONE!

My favorite takeaways from a conference I attended where Jim was
speaking:

- Stop trying to use fear and control to manage behavior.
- Don't pit yourself against the student. If a student is struggling to
  read, the teacher does not shame the student or send them home
  but instead puts a plan in place for the student with extra reading
  time and proximity to a reading specialist. The same approach
  should be used with behaviors and discipline strategies.

> *"If a student is locked in the trunk of the car, don't ask them to drive. Unlock the trunk, and help solve the problem."*

- My favorite quote from Jim is, "If a student is locked in the trunk of the car, don't ask them to drive. Unlock the trunk, and help solve the problem." [75]

The power of one person cannot be underestimated. One teacher can
change the future, and your actions can change the lives of many.

64

15-MINUTE FOCUS
Regulation and Co-Regulation: Accessible Neuroscience and
Connection Strategies that Bring Calm into the Classroom

All You Need is Love?

The more healthy relationships the child has, the more likely they can recover from trauma and thrive. Relationships are the agents of change, and the most powerful therapy is human love.

– Dr. Bruce Perry

Dr. Perry and the Beatles have it right! Co-regulation is about changing brains, but we cannot change those brains if a student doesn't trust us. We cannot successfully break down their defensive barriers and eliminate problematic coping mechanisms unless students feel we are on their side and genuinely care about them. An overall feeling of unconditional positive regard is important in the school setting. We need to teach, model, talk about, and explain that no matter what a student does, we will still accept them.

One of the best examples of love in action is Kansas principal James Moffett who taught me the following: It's about forgiveness. We want students to release any burdens of shame they carry for mistakes they have made. Once a student has learned a lesson, we need to send the message that we are not holding on to their mistakes. We can accept students 100% of the time—love is not a budgetary item. This doesn't mean we let them get away with things. It means we love them enough to hold them to a higher standard. When they know they are loved, they will come back and accept help and support.

Principal Moffett is famous for saying, "What's love got to do with it? Everything." Our actions and decisions should be based on love and connection, not on what is easy for the adult. Showing love doesn't mean we are permissive, but it's also not being overly strict. We must come to the middle with firm compassion, balance structure with nurturance, and connect before we correct.

Principal Moffett teaches that we can implement firm compassion by bringing students closer when something doesn't go right. Punishment will not get to the root cause or help students heal. It may feel counterintuitive for some to bring a student closer emotionally and physically during dysregulation, but increased connection with caring adults is exactly what they need. Every child should have a person in their school who is watching out for them. When students know we sit at the

15-MINUTE FOCUS
Regulation and Co-Regulation: Accessible Neuroscience and
Connection Strategies that Bring Calm into the Classroom

65

table on their behalf, they will rise to the occasion. When the environment changes, behaviors change.[76]

I am not saying any of this is easy. Connection is harder with some kids than others. But I believe there is always a way to reach out and love.

Source: Adapted from Coffee and Quotes (2020) posted on Facebook

How Healthy Attachment Calms the Nervous System

We are not survival of the fittest. We are survival of the nurtured... those who are nurtured best, survive best.

– Louis Cozolino

66

15-MINUTE FOCUS
Regulation and Co-Regulation: Accessible Neuroscience and
Connection Strategies that Bring Calm into the Classroom

Emotional pain is felt as physical pain. It hurts. When we experience emotional pain, the most adaptive thing humans can do is seek refuge in relationships and reassurance with those we trust to feel better. Students will seek soothing in many ways. Additionally, there are many threats to creating healthy attachment,[77] such as:

- Unrelieved pain
- Abuse and/or neglect
- Multiple caretakers
- Invasive and/or painful medical procedures
- Postpartum depression
- Separation

We are born into this life, completely vulnerable and dependent on safe adults to meet our needs and keep us alive. When those needs are consistently met, it helps us build secure attachments. It teaches us we can depend on others, the world is safe, and that someone is looking out for us. This also teaches us when difficult times come, we can wait, find a way to get our needs met, and everything will be okay. But if a child has not received comfort and consistency from a regulated adult, they have difficulty regulating their own emotions and impulses.

Educators have a significant influence on the climate and culture in their buildings. If a student trusts their teacher (or any safe adult in the school), they will feel safe. Once safety is established, the doors to learning are open. Safety always comes first. Without it, the brain's only goal is to survive perceived threats through flight, fight, freeze, and fawn responses.[78] Safety and attachment go hand-in-hand. Building attachment sets us up for a lifetime of healthy relationships and strong self-regulating abilities.[79]

The following graphic shows the student resilience-building cycle through the application of relational practices with the educator. The critical components in building resilience and successfully navigating academics are healthy relationships and the ability to self-regulate. The educator has great power, which is why ultimately, you are **the** strategy.

15-MINUTE FOCUS
Regulation and Co-Regulation: Accessible Neuroscience and
Connection Strategies that Bring Calm into the Classroom

67

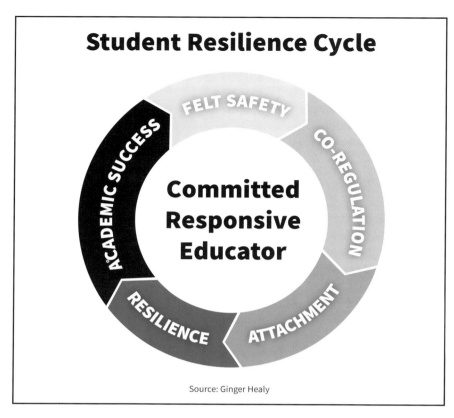

Student Resilience Cycle

Committed Responsive Educator

FELT SAFETY · CO-REGULATION · ATTACHMENT · RESILIENCE · ACADEMIC SUCCESS

Source: Ginger Healy

Consistent, compassionate caregiving helps children learn to modulate immediate emotions and develop long-term self-control. Students need us to notice them and to see them fully. This is more than paying attention. It is sensitive attunement to how they're feeling. **You** are the strategy and can help them understand, accept, and learn to manage their feelings.

Strategies

Dual Drawing: Share a sheet of paper and set the timer for one minute. When the time starts, draw a line or shape and then pass it to the student, who adds a line or shape. Pass the paper back and forth until the timer runs out. Give your joint artwork a title and display it. For older students, you may want to do this with sentences to form a story.

68

15-MINUTE FOCUS
Regulation and Co-Regulation: Accessible Neuroscience and
Connection Strategies that Bring Calm into the Classroom

Be a Thermostat Not a Thermometer: A thermostat sets the temperature and can regulate and adjust based on the environment. A thermometer just reads the temperature. Use this metaphor to respond rather than react to students' emotions. If we react to the environment and mirror their dysregulation, we cannot properly respond. However, if we respond like a thermostat, we can adjust, model regulation, and control those mirror neurons. If the student starts dysregulating, stay regulated. Be the thermostat. Be the strategy.

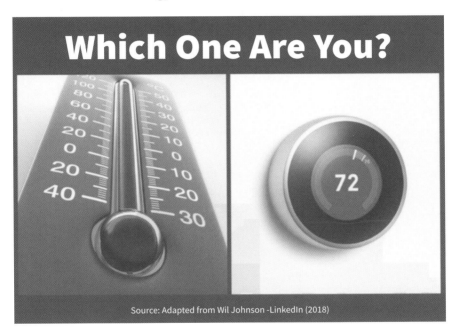

Source: Adapted from Wil Johnson -LinkedIn (2018)

Student Story

After years as a school administrator, Jim Sporleder noticed that students often struggle in school because they experience fear of failure and embarrassment. Students don't want to look stupid in front of their peers. When Jim spoke with students one-on-one, they repeatedly told him they felt like they were the only ones in the class who didn't know the answers. When Jim asked the students what the educators could do to help, they shared that when teachers write the assignment on the board, they can't always follow it and get lost and frustrated. Inevitably the teacher will say with good intent, "If you need help, come see me."

15-MINUTE FOCUS
Regulation and Co-Regulation: Accessible Neuroscience and
Connection Strategies that Bring Calm into the Classroom

69

Every student told Jim there was no way they would ever go to the teacher's desk and ask for help because the other students would see them and think they were stupid. But if the teacher came to their desk and said, "This looks hard, let me help," the students would overwhelmingly accept help. His motto: *Teach from your feet, not from the seat.*

15-MINUTE FOCUS
Regulation and Co-Regulation: Accessible Neuroscience and
Connection Strategies that Bring Calm into the Classroom

Think about the questions below and how you would personally answer them. These answers will make you a better educator by knowing what helps ground you. Ask the same questions to your students to get to know them better and strengthen your relationship with them. The student's answers can be a guide to their regulation.

QUESTIONS to CONSIDER

1. Who are the people who anchor me?

2. What places feel safe and comfortable?

3. What things or objects ground me?

4. Are there days and times I feel more centered?

KEY POINTS

- Shame can prevent students from being open to your support. Be ready to reconnect as soon as the student is ready.

- When we are isolated and disconnected, we are vulnerable. Relational glue keeps our species alive, and love is a relational superglue.[80]

- Bonding behaviors decrease when adults are overwhelmed or in distress. The adult's capacity to give and meet student needs is diminished with increasing threat and distress.[81] We can't escape stress, but we can learn how to deal with it properly.

- Pausing before reacting is a key skill to master. It has a direct connection to regulation. Bruce Perry teaches that regulation gives us the ability to put time and thought between a feeling and an action.

- Developing caring, responsive relationships with students increases trust, which then leads to more success in teaching self-regulation skills.

15-MINUTE FOCUS
Regulation and Co-Regulation: Accessible Neuroscience and
Connection Strategies that Bring Calm into the Classroom

71

15-MINUTE FOCUS
Regulation and Co-Regulation: Accessible Neuroscience and
Connection Strategies that Bring Calm into the Classroom

6 Practical Ways to Create Calming Spaces

A soothing space or regulation area can be used to deescalate emotions or anxiety before a child gets too overwhelmed. It is a space within a school setting that can allow students to access various tools and techniques to combat nervous system overload or daily stress. The room provides a quiet, comfortable space for students to reset and co-regulate while learning self-regulation skills. They are meant to help children struggling to process senses and feelings specifically. In short, it is a safe space before, during, and after dysregulation.

Create a Calm Kit: Up and Down-Regulation

A calm kit contains tools to help children (and adults) regulate their emotions when they feel dysregulated. The name "calm kit" (or calm room), however, is misleading. A better name would be "regulation kit" because the goal isn't always to be calm. I would rather we put focus on being steady, balanced, and regulated. Calm doesn't answer the underlying need; it may appease the adult but doesn't heal in the long-term. Expecting a child to be calm may cause harm to the child's nervous system. A child may calm down or act calm to avoid punishment out of fear, but inside, they may be frozen due to dysregulation and need activation to sync with their nervous system. So our priority needs to shift from expecting calm to working toward regulation. We do that through activation when we co-regulate. There is both up-regulation and down-regulation.

Up-regulation is energizing regulation that arouses us when we are distracted, tired, or depressed. In this situation, we need tools and skills to help us engage, stay alert, and focus on the present. If someone is stuck in freeze, they often need up-regulation in order to come back to a feeling of

15-MINUTE FOCUS
Regulation and Co-Regulation: Accessible Neuroscience and
Connection Strategies that Bring Calm into the Classroom

73

safety. Fawn responses are tricky when it comes to knowing how best to help a student.

The fawn response involves both fight/flight and freeze at the same time. Those whose natural response is to make everything ok (fawn) by doing whatever they perceive others want (fight/flight) suppress and deny their own needs (freeze)in order to survive. It depends on the situation regarding whether up vs down-regulation should be used when a student is in a fawn response but should always be focused on creating felt safety.

Down-regulation is calming regulation. It quiets our nervous system when we are overactivated, overstimulated, and distracted. We need tools and skills to help us become in tune, focused, and feel settled. Down-regulation is appropriate for both fight and flight reactions. Regulation kits and safe spaces can help in both up- and down-regulation scenarios.

Build your kit with items such as:

- Coloring supplies
- Glitter wands
- Oil and water drip timers
- Breathing prompts (with pictures for younger children)
- Pinwheels
- Bubbles
- Visual timer
- Squishies
- Fidgets
- Silicone sponges
- Pipe cleaners
- Noise-canceling headphones
- Pulse oximeter

Safe Spaces

A relaxation room, a zen den, a cozy corner, a peaceful place—call it what you want. These spaces are meant to provide a safe spot for students to co-regulate with an adult and practice self-regulation skills. These spaces

74

15-MINUTE FOCUS
Regulation and Co-Regulation: Accessible Neuroscience and
Connection Strategies that Bring Calm into the Classroom

aren't meant for free play or escaping class or assignments. Typically, one student may visit the space at a time for 5-10 minutes and then return to class. It's not a time out either where a teacher sends a student there as a consequence.

The space should always have a regulated, trauma-informed adult available to co-regulate with a child, who knows what to do when a student is in complete dysregulation. The staff needs to know how to help a child shift from their downstairs brain to their upstairs brain through co-regulation.

Additionally, assisting staff need to know what to do if the student cannot co-regulate and they need backup. These spaces are not seclusion or isolation rooms. School administration should explain the purpose of the room, its benefits, and the available tools. Rules for use should be posted for all teachers, staff, and students.

Rules for Calming/Regulation Kits and Spaces

- **Rule 1:** The use of regulation tools in these spaces must be taught and encouraged. Do not assume students automatically know how to use each item. It is also important to help kids understand what will help and what they should do when they feel dysregulated.
- **Rule 2:** Students need the freedom to choose which tools they use. Not everything in the space or kit will work for each student. Learning what soothes individual students is an important part of the process. Encourage students to experiment with a variety of tools and tactile sensations: soft, firm, stretchy, bendy, fuzzy, prickly, weighted, etc.
- **Rule 3:** Students need the freedom to access regulation tools whenever they need them. Kits and spaces should be readily available during instruction, not just during free time or recess. They should also not be used as a punishment for misbehavior or a reward for free time.[82]

The following list contains tools able to be used in a classroom setting, school counseling office, or any safe spot in a school building. Having a good mix of tactile, vestibular, and proprioceptive options enables students to find what they need that works best for them during

15-MINUTE FOCUS
Regulation and Co-Regulation: Accessible Neuroscience and
Connection Strategies that Bring Calm into the Classroom

75

moments of dysregulation. Engaging the hidden senses (vestibular and proprioceptive) helps children feel safe, in control, and able to return to classroom work. [83]

Tools and Materials for Regulation Spaces

Items for tactile/touch input and fine motor skills (these items bring awareness to touch, which is needed during times of disconnection):

- Fidgets (e.g., poppers, spinners)
- Squishies, goo, silly putty
- Spray bottles, silicone sponges
- Shaving cream, kinetic sand, playdough
- Stickers, pipe cleaners

Items for body input, movement, and gross motor skills (these proprioceptive and vestibular tools help students find what feels "just right" to regulate and move from their downstairs brain back into their upstairs brain):

- Weighted blanket, wrap, or lap pad
- Mini-trampoline
- Wall push poster
- Crash pad
- Plushies-pillows
- Therabands
- Swing
- Wobble seat
- Chair bands

Snacks and water bottles can also be a part of a safe space. One of the common reasons for dysregulation is dehydration, hunger, and fatigue. Having allergen-free snacks and protein-based snacks can release neurotransmitters and help prevent depression and anxiety.

76

15-MINUTE FOCUS
Regulation and Co-Regulation: Accessible Neuroscience and
Connection Strategies that Bring Calm into the Classroom

Safety as a Strategy

Safety comes first. Everyone must feel safe. We must create the feeling of physical, emotional, and mental safety. Safety is not a thought in the mind but an experience in the body. Healing can't be rushed, but you can help it progress dramatically. Children who feel safe are free to heal and become secure, trusting children. Providing an atmosphere of "felt safety" disarms the primitive brain and reduces fear. It is a critical first step toward helping the child heal and grow.[84]

I once spoke with a teacher who was frustrated with a student for refusing to help bring supplies to the classroom from school basement. The student was terrified at the request, and the teacher was annoyed with non-compliance. To the teacher, there was nothing wrong with the basement. But to the student who had experienced abuse in a cold dark place, the basement was never going to feel safe, even though it technically was.

We must trust the child and understand they need repetitive moments of true felt safety to help manage those triggers that set off a danger warning in their limbic system/mid-brain area. Most importantly, create a safe atmosphere with the positive, caring, knowledgeable staff who work there. Staff members can create felt safety in a classroom or any space by:

- Be attuned and present while holding space for student emotions. This means that we provide emotional room for the student to accept their feelings without judgment and reflect those feelings back to the student to help them feel seen and felt.

- Avoid sarcasm, watch body language, and use a friendly and soothing volume and tone of voice. Use simple words or language they understand and respond attentively and kindly to your student's words and actions. Interact playfully by physically matching or mirroring a student's voice and behavior.

- Announce upcoming transitions and plans to aid children in preparing for the impending change. Predictability, routine, and structure help students feel safe. A daily schedule is essential; provide a visual schedule for students with reading deficits or ESL/ELL needs.

15-MINUTE FOCUS
Regulation and Co-Regulation: Accessible Neuroscience and
Connection Strategies that Bring Calm into the Classroom

77

Creating Physically and Emotionally Safe Environments as Buffers for Children

Source: Ginger Healy

In the center is the child. The next layer is an adult (educator or caregiver) who surrounds the child—notice the arms in a hug formation—providing a buffer against adversities. The adult can be a cushion and help heal the child by being regulated, asking for and accepting help, embracing self-compassion, and managing their stressors.

78

15-MINUTE FOCUS
Regulation and Co-Regulation: Accessible Neuroscience and
Connection Strategies that Bring Calm into the Classroom

The adult creates an ongoing safe environment that safeguards them both through:

- Co-regulation with an attitude of playfulness, acceptance, and a balance of structure and nurturance (brain-based discipline strategies used)
- The use of available regulation tools understood by both adult and child
- Accommodations such as adjustable lighting, movement breaks, and flexible seating (sensory-safe environment) depending on the child's regulation needs
- Hydration breaks, healthy snacks, and nutritious meals
- Friendly noise levels, headphones available, adult avoids yelling, pleasant tones used for transition notification
- Allowances made for mistakes, opportunities for "do-overs" (adult leads by example, apologizing when necessary and discussing their own mistakes)
- Clutter-free physical space
- Visual schedules posted for predictability
- Allowing the child to participate in the creation of the schedule
- Adult remaining in close proximity to the child but does not hover
- Adult is attuned to child's needs and responds with empathy and curiosity (especially surrounding the child's behavior)

The community can buffer the adults in the child's life with support and resources, which then strengthens the adult(s) to be better able to support and buffer the child.

Strategies

The following are all excellent strategies for bottom-up regulation and work best when they are modeled and done in tandem. Breathing exercises are a great proactive group regulation tool and can be led by a student.

Intentional Deep Breathing is essential for both emotional and physical well-being. Deep breathing is a powerful way to regulate and reduce

15-MINUTE FOCUS
Regulation and Co-Regulation: Accessible Neuroscience and
Connection Strategies that Bring Calm into the Classroom

79

cortisol. Our lungs are covered with nerves that extend to our nervous system. Long, slow breaths relax us because they reach the lower lobes of our lungs, where nerves connect to the digestive system and send the message to rest and digest. When the breath rises to exhale, a message is released to slow the heart down and send oxygen to the brain, calming us down while activating important parts of the brain. Don't forget to make each exhale much longer than the inhale.

For **Volcanic Breathing,** tell students to bring their hands together (palms facing each other) and form a volcano on the inhale. On the exhale, ask them to explode their hands, arms, and breath wide into the air. Repeat.

In **Rose and Candle**, have students cross their arms over their chest. In one hand, have them visualize holding a rose, and in the other hand, tell them to hold an imaginary lit candle. Direct them to smell the rose on the inhale and blow out the candle on the exhale. Repeat.

For the **Hot Pizza** exercise, tell students to pretend to pull their favorite warm food out of the oven. First, they should inhale and smell the deliciousness, then notice how hot it is and cool it off by exhaling long and slow. Repeat.

For the **Focus** exercise, students should choose something specific to notice with one of their senses. For example, they can pick a color and name all the objects in the room with that color or listen intently to a particular sound they hear and describe it in detail. It can be done with a smell they notice or something they can touch in the room. This grounding strategy encourages someone to come back to their body and become more aware of their surroundings when they feel disconnected.

In **54321**, students use their five senses and name five things they see, four things they hear, three things they smell, two things they can touch, and one thing they taste. The order doesn't matter. Switch it up and pair different numbers with different senses when you repeat until the student feels more present and aware.

Student Story

When Dr. Dustin Springer, principal of Gray Hawk Elementary, opened his new school, he felt it was critical to have a Regulation Room for the

80

15-MINUTE FOCUS
Regulation and Co-Regulation: Accessible Neuroscience and
Connection Strategies that Bring Calm into the Classroom

adults where they could go when dysregulated, struggling with a personal or student issue, or just needed a safe place where they could step away for a breather. This safe space allows adults to meet their own social and emotional needs and become aware of their brain and body states to serve their students best.

Dr. Springer said, "This room lets our adults know that we are here to support one another and recognize that we all experience things that activate us. I wanted to normalize the idea that we all need time to regulate."

Gray Hawk's staff "Zen Den" includes comfortable seating, a stuffed animal that can be heated or cooled and used as a compress, positive affirmations, and other inspirational literature. It also includes a Bluetooth speaker to connect to phones for use with the Calm app or regulating music along with paper, pens, markers, and other writing instruments for "brain dumps." Dr. Springer said, "We have aromatics in the room because lavender and vanilla scents can be regulating. Recently, one of our paraeducators placed a mirror in the room because our faces communicate so much to our students, so she felt it was important to "check ourselves" to see what nonverbal cues we may be giving off."

Dr. Springer also shared that in every classroom in his building, there is an "amygdala re-set/peace corner." The school also has what he calls a "transitional safe space" for students who need more than the classroom regulation corner can provide that lets students transition in and out of the classroom during dysregulation. Dr. Springer meets with all staff to train them on each item in the peace corner, transition space, and staff zen den to teach brain-based co-regulation strategies and correct implementation of each tool in each room. He says the results have been phenomenal. "We have a happy, resilient staff. A regulated brain and body is one of the greatest gifts we can share with our adults—and ultimately our students. Remaining focused on that more than the content has proven to be vital to our success."

15-MINUTE FOCUS
Regulation and Co-Regulation: Accessible Neuroscience and
Connection Strategies that Bring Calm into the Classroom

81

QUESTIONS to CONSIDER

1. What smells can I incorporate into our space to ease anxiety and encourage a mindful state of learning?

2. What lighting accommodations can be incorporated into the space to promote alertness and focus?

3. What type of flexible seating can I incorporate that allows movement and the ability to work collaboratively while fostering creativity and critical thinking skills?

4. How can the staff and I add to the environment through our nervous system states?

KEY POINTS

- Deep breathing is essential for students who tend to hold their breath or breathe quickly and shallowly when in survival mode. Controlling our breath reduces fear and centers us during times of overwhelm.

- Creating an environment of physical and emotional safety is essential for EVERYONE in our schools. One of the very best ways to create a safe environment is through routine and predictability.

- Unpredictability over time creates toxic stress because it is a form of neglect and can lead to feelings of traumatization.[85]

- Emotionally and physically safe environments where students are connected and regulated allow for the greatest opportunity to achieve academic success.

82

15-MINUTE FOCUS
Regulation and Co-Regulation: Accessible Neuroscience and
Connection Strategies that Bring Calm into the Classroom

7 Supporting Yourself and Avoiding Burnout

Are you experiencing any of the following?

- Emotional exhaustion from caring too much for too long
- Depersonalization- going through the motions, becoming robotic
- Decreased sense of accomplishment and feeling that nothing you do makes a difference

Experiencing burnout is extremely common, and educators are at particular risk. Educators give, give, give until they have nothing left, and then continue to give. Educators continuously attend to the needs of others, dismiss their own stress, and deem it inconsequential. However, educator stress is extremely consequential. Burnout is strongly linked to negative impacts on health, relationships, and work resulting in incomplete stress response cycles accumulating in their bodies.[86]

Completing the Stress Cycle

Stress is the neurobiological and physiological shift that happens in your body when you encounter a threat—an evolutionarily adaptive response that helps us cope. If stress is constant, it is easy to get stuck in the stress cycle and leave the body soaked in stress hormones.

In moments when you feel "stuck," you need to do something to let your body know you are safe. You can be well during stressful times. Wellness is not a state of being but a state of action. The following are seven actions that can help relieve stress hormones and complete the stress cycle:[87]

15-MINUTE FOCUS
Regulation and Co-Regulation: Accessible Neuroscience and
Connection Strategies that Bring Calm into the Classroom

83

1. Exercise
2. Deep breathing exercises
3. Social interaction
4. Laughter
5. Affection
6. Crying
7. Creative expression

Embracing Self-Compassion

Source:@decade2doodles (2022)

You can't be compassionate to others if you aren't compassionate with yourself first. Self-compassion is the first step to healing shame and requires us to give ourselves understanding rather than ignoring our pain.[88] Self-compassion changes the brain. A compassionate brain is open and available to shift, take in new information, and develop more connections in the brain, body, and with others.

You can't be regulated all the time; it's not humanly possible. We will always encounter challenges and we will always make mistakes, and that is okay. As we grow, change, and repair mistakes, we build resilience. Our brains and bodies will more quickly ease into regulation the more we practice self-regulation through implementing regulation tools and strategies and the more we co-regulate with others. The more we repair the ruptures, the more easily we regulate and re-wire our brains into positive neural pathways away from dysregulation. We can modulate

84

15-MINUTE FOCUS
Regulation and Co-Regulation: Accessible Neuroscience and
Connection Strategies that Bring Calm into the Classroom

emotions rather than "flip our lids." We do this through practicing self-compassion.

Mantras for self-compassion might be:

- This is hard, and I am doing the best I can.
- I feel really overwhelmed right now.
- I must be really hurting to have reacted the way I did.
- I am not alone in this. Others are struggling as I am.
- Being human is hard.

Self-compassion moves our nervous system from a reactive state to an open one. We go from feeling tight and constricted to open and curious. The more we shift to being open and receptive, the more we create the neurobiology that supports regulation. **This is so needed in order to continue successfully in this work with students. It's not easy; we often get stuck in shame when exercising self-compassion.**

There are three ways to move from shame into a state of self-compassion: connection, rest, and compassion.

- Connection is nourishment. We are wired for connection as a basic biological need, and loneliness is a form of starvation.
- Rest is medicine. Rest includes sleep, as well as switching from one activity to another.
- And finally, compassion. You cannot be courageous without self-care. You cannot express compassion without self-compassion.[89]

Self-Care and Community Care

Self-care and community care are inextricably linked. Self-care can only go so far without a community to provide when you are not at your best. Proper self-care does not look like the hyper-individualism we have been taught. In other words, there's no community care versus self-care. Rather, the two complement each other, and both are necessary for individual and collective well-being.[90]

Self-care isn't about bubble baths and chocolate. There is a difference between short-term self-soothing and caring for ourselves in an

15-MINUTE FOCUS
Regulation and Co-Regulation: Accessible Neuroscience and
Connection Strategies that Bring Calm into the Classroom

85

intentional, healing way. If you are having any of the following symptoms, you are overdue for care:

- Intrusive thoughts and memories
- Avoiding feelings
- Avoiding the students you work with
- Anger
- Anxiety/depression
- Feeling numb
- Withdrawal
- Difficulty sleeping
- Irritability

Self-care requires a bubble of protection from others who value your well-being as highly as you do. Band-Aids won't work; they are after-care and not a sustainable framework for healing. Instead, focus on prevention and nurture your body, mind, and spirit. Reflect, foster awareness, and commit to yourself. Be authentic and honest about what you truly need, no matter how uncomfortable it feels.

The cure for burnout isn't just about personal self-care. It's all of us caring for each other.[91] We need to pick each other up. We need community care. Community care consists of the collective efforts we make to be healthy and happy. We need to connect, exchange support, and share resources. We need to show up, create space for each other, and create dependable relationships.

Practicing community care can look like:

- Cooking or cleaning for a loved one who is going through a tough time
- Carpooling
- Asking for help from your support system when you need it (and reciprocating it)
- Getting to know your neighbors, co-workers, and community members (grow your circle of support)

Moving toward wellness is a collective, collaborative effort. In working together to help ensure others' needs are met, we are likely to feel well both individually and as a community.[92]

15-MINUTE FOCUS
Regulation and Co-Regulation: Accessible Neuroscience and
Connection Strategies that Bring Calm into the Classroom

Roadblocks to Regulation: Blocked Care and Blocked Trust

One of the biggest precursors for burnout is blocked care. When you give and receive nothing in return, it becomes draining to the point that you may feel hopeless. When a child feels unsafe due to early adversities, they develop a skewed internal working model (belief about themselves), which causes them to jump to self-preservation. They reject bids for connection and relationship, no matter how safe and positive. They do everything they can to avoid trusting anyone so their trust will never be broken. This is called blocked trust. It doesn't matter if you are the gentlest human in the school; they can't handle your compassionate attempts at caregiving. They will block you, and after being repeatedly rejected, you can find yourself having **compassion fatigue** and not able to care or give any more of yourself. This is called blocked care.[94]

This is not a conscious decision for the child; they don't wake up planning to torture the teacher through constant dismissive behavior. Their brains are reacting from the limbic system to help them stay safe and survive. In their attempt to survive, their body releases adrenaline, which tells them to run away from you, fight you, or ignore you.

It becomes problematic when bids for a positive connection with the teacher are rebuffed. While educators understand on a cognitive level that it's not their fault if a child pushes them away, it can feel exhausting, deflating, and overwhelming.

The teacher may be doing all the right things, but when that child's neurobiology reacts in unpleasant ways, the adult can be the one to block the care. In this situation, the teacher may start thinking *I hate my job. I don't like this kid. I cannot do this anymore.*

This is when the teacher needs help. And it can be particularly challenging when the adult's early childhood adversities have created an internal model signaling and tricking them into thinking they are terrible teachers, the child is bad, or they need to get away. However, there is good news: We can unblock what has been blocked!

Dr. Daniel Hughes, clinical psychologist, author, and president of the Dyadic Developmental Psychotherapy Institute (DDPI), developed an attachment and brain-based parenting approach as an effective way

15-MINUTE FOCUS
Regulation and Co-Regulation: Accessible Neuroscience and
Connection Strategies that Bring Calm into the Classroom

87

for caregivers to communicate with and care for children who have experienced trauma. The P.A.C.E attitude enhances the child's sense of safety and increases their trust. P.A.C.E. can be applied both in the classroom and at home to create a safe and therapeutic environment that will help children heal. P.A.C.E. is ideal for blocked care.

- **P is for Playfulness**: Use play to decrease stress and defuse situations. Playfulness increases hope, gives confidence about the future, awakens a positive point of view, reduces shame, and builds trust and safety.

- **A is for Acceptance**: Blend limit setting with empathy and use discipline in the spirit of teaching while keeping relationships safe and intact. When educators can correct and maintain positive connections, they embody this acceptance and help students learn emotional regulation.

- **C is for Curiosity**: Curiosity without judgment conveys the intention to understand and assist students in understanding as well. With curiosity, the goal is to find the stressful thought, feeling, perception, or motive which could only be expressed through behavior. The student is less likely to engage in a behavior again because they understand where it is coming from and can then meet the need in a different way.

- **E is for Empathy**: Empathy enables students to feel compassion from the teacher in the same way curiosity helps students feel understood. With empathy, students do not deal with distress alone, especially when we stay with them and provide support when they need it the most.[93]

The following self-examination questions work well when working with students experiencing blocked care.

- How can I get to know this student better and find some common ground?
- Who does this student trust and how, and how can we all work together for the betterment of the student?
- How can I better understand this student and their struggles?
- How can I instill hope in this student?

88

15-MINUTE FOCUS
Regulation and Co-Regulation: Accessible Neuroscience and
Connection Strategies that Bring Calm into the Classroom

Strategies

Set Boundaries: Sometimes, in this work, we become too accessible. You can always be a safe person, but you can't be all things to all students. This work is therapeutic, but helping with healing doesn't mean conducting therapy. It's important to set boundaries and guide students and families to safe adults and resources. Boundaries allow you to care for yourself and the other person at the same time without trying to solve all their worries. Figure out what is within your control, and don't be afraid to say no when requests exceed your bandwidth or capabilities. Avoid working overtime, leave work at work, ask for help, utilize employee assistance programs, and get support from peers. Be ready for pushback. If you never say "no," others may be surprised when you do.

Get out the paint! Express yourself creatively through painting, sculpting, storytelling, music, crafting—whatever you like. Creative expression helps you tolerate and modulate overwhelming emotions and encourages the release of big emotions that may be stuck. Trying something new and creative uses the part of our brain that shifts us out of being stuck. (This works for students, too!)

Be a contagious example of community care within the school environment:

- Support other staff members by saying thank you or writing a note about positive things you noticed they did.
- Help plan a staff appreciation activity to focus on coming together and team building.
- Set boundaries with work email on the weekends and evenings.
- Let PTA leaders and school admin know that educators would love to be loved and then give specific suggestions they may have never thought of.

Here are some ideas that other schools have used:

- Breakfast or Lunch service once a month
- Pick a day to leave early
- Bowling Night
- Book Club
- Potluck at the Park

15-MINUTE FOCUS
Regulation and Co-Regulation: Accessible Neuroscience and
Connection Strategies that Bring Calm into the Classroom

89

- Birthday Surprises
- Dress Down Days

Student Story

I once had the honor and privilege of speaking at the same conference as my hero, Nadine Burke Harris. As I fangirled during our virtual conference, she told a story I would never forget. As the Surgeon General of California when the pandemic hit, she was understandably overwhelmed, overworked, and over-stressed. The pandemic wasn't ending anytime soon. One day, her daughter approached her and said, "Mommy, you lost your giggle!" This was a wake-up call.

She spoke about the toll caring takes on those working in helping professions. She ended her speech by saying, "You know that metaphor of putting the oxygen mask on yourself before putting it on your child? Pfft! Forget the oxygen mask! You need scuba gear with several full tanks of oxygen and a dive team! You need a plan, tools, resources, equipment, training, and most of all, lots of support."

She paused.

"Don't put yourself at risk. Don't go underwater alone. Don't lose your giggle."

I will never forget her words or her sincere plea. Truly walking the walk, she resigned from her huge, amazing job shortly after to go in search of her giggle.

90

15-MINUTE FOCUS
Regulation and Co-Regulation: Accessible Neuroscience and
Connection Strategies that Bring Calm into the Classroom

QUESTIONS to CONSIDER

1. What are some specific ways I can work on completing the stress cycle in my life?

2. In what ways can I express more self-compassion?

3. What opportunities for community care within the school can I implement?

KEY POINTS

- Rest is essential when it comes to regulation because emotions are integrated and processed when we sleep. After co-regulation, you may find you are exhausted and drained. Pay attention to how you feel.

- Perfectionism is an impossible goal. The opposite of self-criticism and toxic perfectionism is self-compassion. Be gentle with yourself. You are worth it.

- Think of how you would treat a small child you adore. You are that child, and you can show up for yourself in the same way.

- Neurobiological self-care and burnout prevention include caring for physical health, getting adequate sleep, moving through grief, getting mental breaks, and expressing gratitude.

- You don't have to set yourself on fire to keep others warm.[95]

15-MINUTE FOCUS
Regulation and Co-Regulation: Accessible Neuroscience and
Connection Strategies that Bring Calm into the Classroom

91

15-MINUTE FOCUS
Regulation and Co-Regulation: Accessible Neuroscience and
Connection Strategies that Bring Calm into the Classroom

8

Supporting Parents, Caregivers, and Families

Family engagement is one of the most powerful predictors of children's development, educational attainment, and success in school and life.[96]

As a therapist, I always say that one hour once a week in therapy is not as powerful in healing and growing a child as the other 167 hours in the week, when a child spends most of that time at home and school. Educators supporting families supports the child. And families supporting educators supports the child.

Bridging the Gap Between Schools and Families

What would happen if schools and families were empowered to work well together? Family engagement is a core component of any intentional effort to provide equitable, excellent educational opportunities for children. Schools understand the need for family engagement programs but face barriers, including time, training, accessibility, and funding. Even when those roadblocks are overcome, parents and caregivers don't always feel welcome at the school, especially if they are members of marginalized communities.

The following are potential ways schools can bridge gaps and create stronger relationships with parents and caregivers:

Host parent/caregiver education nights that provide dinner, transportation, and childcare, if possible. Caregivers can be given information and taught the brain science of regulation—how children learn to regulate themselves, and what caregivers can do to encourage self-regulation through co-regulation.

15-MINUTE FOCUS
Regulation and Co-Regulation: Accessible Neuroscience and
Connection Strategies that Bring Calm into the Classroom

93

Educators can do things to establish relationships with parents/caregivers (individually and through schoolwide meetings/programming). If the tone is welcoming and builds trust, the parents/caregivers will be more likely to partner with educators and learn regulation tools and interventions.

Schools with programs that meet families' basic needs (food distribution, access to wrap-around services, adult education/job skills & job finding assistance) are moving obstacles out of families' ways. This enables parents to have more time and energy to devote to learning regulation tools to help their children. Then, participation in parenting classes is more likely.

Other ideas:

- Work and volunteer opportunities for parents/caregivers
- Invite community leaders to meet with parents/caregivers at school
- Time on school grounds for parent coffee chats, support groups, or other activities
- Teacher caregiver community service opportunities

Adapting Classroom Strategies for Home

We can modify the environment to decrease stressors impacting a child's behavior by creating a physically and emotionally safe environment both in school and at home. Whether an educator or caregiver, adults are the best strategy for children.

One of the best ways to intervene when a child becomes dysregulated is the Re-Set Process developed for the school setting and created by educator, administrator, consultant, staff developer, and author Dyane Carrere. This Re-Set Process can be easily adapted to the home environment or any location the parent/caregiver is with the child to help a child move from downstairs brain to upstairs brain. (Meltdown at the grocery store? Asking for a friend.)

94

15-MINUTE FOCUS
Regulation and Co-Regulation: Accessible Neuroscience and
Connection Strategies that Bring Calm into the Classroom

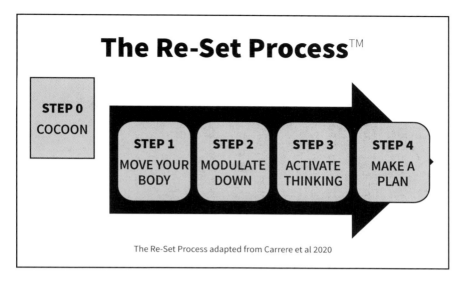

The Re-Set Process adapted from Carrere et al 2020

Here is a simplified summary:

- Establish Safety: Helping a child feel safe always comes first.
    - Keep language to a minimum
    - Provide comfort items (drink of water, weighted blanket)
    - Stay near, but don't hover
    - When the child is ready, get them moving with you. It will burn off stress chemicals, introduce feel-good hormones, and allow the child to tune in to you.

- Move for two minutes:
    - Lunges
    - Wide arm circles
    - Walking

- Transition from large to small movements (to continue burning off stress) for one minute:
    - Stretching
    - Shoulder shrugs
    - Tense and release
    - Deep breaths

15-MINUTE FOCUS
Regulation and Co-Regulation: Accessible Neuroscience and
Connection Strategies that Bring Calm into the Classroom

95

- Activate their brain and get the hemispheres talking to each other for one minute:
  - Doodle
  - Make a list of their favorite things
- Discuss what happened for one minute:
  - Plan for the next time it happens in a non-shameful way
  - Laugh about mistakes everyone made

This whole process only takes a few minutes![97]

As parents/caregivers and educators, if our goal is compliance or obedience, we are communicating a need for control, power over, and relief from the felt chaos in our own nervous systems. If we desire connection when encountering a rough behavior, we can offer time, space, and a felt presence that invites the nervous system inside to rest while we figure it out.

We're All in This Together

Communities can provide schools with a context and environment that can complement and reinforce the values, culture, and learning that schools provide. A solid connection to the community is as important today as it was thousands of years ago. There is a direct relationship between a person's degree of social isolation and risk for physical and mental health problems. Connection gives us a buffer for stress and distress.[98] In this modern era, creating community is challenging when we are mobile, screened up, and disconnected. However, we still need to try and ensure connectedness, a sense of safety, and belonging for everyone.

A person's capacity to connect, be regulated, and regulate others is the glue that keeps families and communities together. Belonging and being loved are core to the human experience. We are a social species meant to be emotionally, socially, and physically interconnected with others.

No one person could be all things for all children. Each person at school and home has a unique set of strengths, and no single person is expected to provide for all the emotional, social, physical, or cognitive needs of a

15-MINUTE FOCUS
Regulation and Co-Regulation: Accessible Neuroscience and
Connection Strategies that Bring Calm into the Classroom

developing child. However, we're meant to work together and distribute caregiving among the many adults in our community.[99]

Strategies

These top-down strategies can work both at home and in the classroom.

Mindful sharing between caregiver and child and teacher and student. For instance:

- Name something that is going well.
- Describe an emotion you felt today.
- Name something you are grateful for.
- Name something you want to do better today.

Invisible ink: Spell one word in the air with a partner related to something they just learned. Have the other partner guess the word. After each round, the speller shares why they picked their word. Switch and repeat.

Junk drawer: Grab an object from the junk drawer and have the child devise a new purpose for that object.

Music scribble: Play a song and have the child scribble what they envision the song would look like in pictures. When finished, they can share their scribbles and name their art.

Tongue talk: Take turns sharing things you've learned while keeping your tongue on the roof of your mouth.

Wink and snap: Wink with one eye and snap the fingers of the opposite hand. Switch.

Traveling shoes: Place an old pair of shoes on the table. Ask the child to imagine where the shoes have been.

Genius dinner: Select several characters, historical figures, or favorite heroes. Pretend all the characters go to dinner. Ask the child to imagine what they eat, what they talk about, and how they would solve the problems of modern times

15-MINUTE FOCUS
Regulation and Co-Regulation: Accessible Neuroscience and
Connection Strategies that Bring Calm into the Classroom

97

Student Story

Hunter's teacher, Miss Vitaly, noticed he often showed up to school tired, hungry, and not ready to learn. She also noticed he wore the same outfit most days, and it needed to be washed. He was often teased by other students for his clothes and messy hair.

Miss Vitaly set up a meeting with Hunter's mother, who shared that his father passed away the previous year, forcing her to work double shifts to provide for Hunter and his siblings. Hunter's mother was ashamed and expressed exhaustion and hopelessness.

Miss Vitaly shared a community resource directory with Hunter's mother with links to programs to help families with heating bills, a food pantry, a clothing swap, and after-school programs for all the children. She also provided Hunter's mom with the phone numbers of other parents in the community who volunteered with the school and family partnership to support families with needs.

After this, Hunter often met with the school social worker to work through his grief and loss. Hunter's grades began to rise, along with his confidence. The community resources helped buffer Hunter's mom, and the school staff helped ease the adversities Hunter and his siblings faced.

98

15-MINUTE FOCUS
Regulation and Co-Regulation: Accessible Neuroscience and
Connection Strategies that Bring Calm into the Classroom

Co-regulation is about the setting in our schools and home. So, consider the environment and ask yourself:

QUESTIONS to CONSIDER

1. Does this setting feel safe for the child?

2. Do the children and adults have input in the environment regarding color, objects, furniture, and schedule?

3. Are the students surrounded by safe adults they trust in this environment?

KEY POINTS

- Each student and family is different. A checklist for supporting families and the needs of a child are entirely individual. One size fits one.

- There will never be a universal response to an interaction or intervention. Not every student will absorb a math lesson or feel the same feelings. In the same way, each family will also have different needs.

- Relationships are the most effective vehicle for learning and meeting needs. Implementation strategies need to be relationally based. Cognitive-based strategy will not work.

15-MINUTE FOCUS
Regulation and Co-Regulation: Accessible Neuroscience and
Connection Strategies that Bring Calm into the Classroom

99

Conclusion

My goals for this book are to help child-serving professionals understand regulation and co-regulation to help children manage their feelings and alleviate dysregulation. Remember: Calm is not the goal. There are times when calm helps a child feel peaceful, but we can't be calm 100% of the time. Don't mistake calm for regulation. A well-behaved child also isn't the goal. A child behaving out of fear while being completely dysregulated and swimming in stress hormones causes harm far beyond a behavior moment. Managing behavioral challenges through punitive discipline is also not the goal. Contrary to popular belief, traditional discipline is not the best way to help children behave better and doesn't work long-term. We must move to brain-based discipline through co-regulation and the tools and strategies that this book outlines.

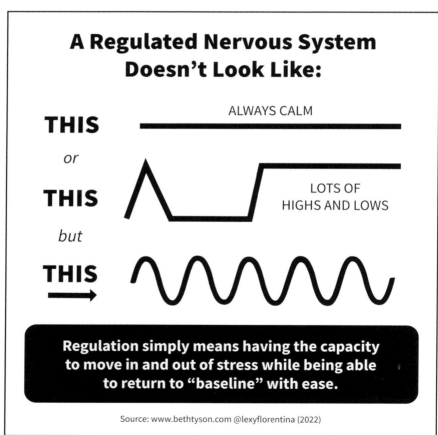

A Regulated Nervous System Doesn't Look Like:

THIS ALWAYS CALM

or

THIS LOTS OF HIGHS AND LOWS

but

THIS →

Regulation simply means having the capacity to move in and out of stress while being able to return to "baseline" with ease.

Source: www.bethtyson.com @lexyflorentina (2022)

100

15-MINUTE FOCUS
Regulation and Co-Regulation: Accessible Neuroscience and
Connection Strategies that Bring Calm into the Classroom

The goal is for us to get comfortable feeling all feelings so we can help children feel theirs and understand what their feelings communicate to them. **The management of all emotions and moving fluidly between them is the goal. The goal is co-regulation.**

Co-regulation doesn't mean a lack of structure, boundaries, expectations, or consequences. Co-regulation is not a reward for misbehavior. Quite the opposite, co-regulation is a higher standard of accountability coupled with compassion. It alleviates the need for students to act out because it keeps them safe inside their bodies. It's the key to ultimately developing self-regulation, which results in better behaviors.

Don't ever forget that when a child is seen, heard, and felt, their nervous systems will settle.

Doing this can be as simple as:

- Being present
- Being attentive
- Being attuned
- Being responsive

And it can start with you. For many children and youth, an educator may be the first adult to hold space, reflect, and feel the depth of their experience.[100] People, not programs, change people.[101] Change begins with co-regulation, which changes the relationship of power between two people and is the core of discipline through a brain-aligned, relational lens. When we share our calming presence to help a child through the storm, we are sharing a sanctuary of safety.[102]

Teachers! Thank you for all you do. So much of what you do is unseen and unappreciated. You are the unsung heroes. Keeping going! You are needed, so very needed! You may not see the fruits of the seeds you plant, but I promise you make a difference. Students may not remember all the lessons taught I can guarantee they remember how you make them feel. You are investing in the most valuable commodity possible. You are investing in the future; the payoff is immeasurable!

15-MINUTE FOCUS
Regulation and Co-Regulation: Accessible Neuroscience and
Connection Strategies that Bring Calm into the Classroom

101

Notes

1, 4, 5, 7, 61, 69   Delahooke, Mona. *Beyond Behaviors: Using Brain Science and Compassion to Understand and Solve Children's Behavioral Challenges*. Eau Claire, Wi, Pesi Publishers, 2019.

2   *Emotional regulation & ADHD: What you need to know*. Life Skills Advocate. (2022, November 26). https://lifeskillsadvocate.com/blog/emotional-regulation-adhd-what-you-need-to-know

3   Mahler, K. (2021, October 14). *Modern Emotion Regulation supports for Neurodivergent Learners*. Kelly Mahler. https://www.kelly-mahler.com/resources/blog/modern-emotion-regulation-supports-for-neurodivergent-learners-are-you-keeping-with-the-times/

6   Sadin, Melissa, and Nathan Levy. *Teachers' Guide to Trauma: 20 Things Kids with Trauma Wish Their Teachers Knew*. Monroe Township, Nj, Nathan Levy Books, LLC., 2018.

8, 76   Perry, Bruce Duncan, and Maia Szalavitz. *The Boy Who Was Raised as a Dog : And Other Stories from a Child Psychiatrist's Notebook : What Traumatized Children Can Teach Us about Loss, Love, and Healing*. 2006. New York, Basic Books, 2017.

9, 51, 57, 60, 64, 67, 72, 96   Carrere, Dyane Lewis, et al. *The Re-Set Process: Trauma-Informed Behavior Strategies*. Newburyport, Brookes Publishing, 2020.

10, 48   Edwards, Allison, and National Center For Youth Issues. *Flooded: A Brain-Based Guide to Help Children Regulate Emotions*. Chattanooga, Tn, National Center For Youth Issues, 2021.

11   Bowlby, John. *Attachment and Loss*. Vol. 1, New York, Basic Books, 1969.

12, 15, 68   Buckwalter, Karen Doyle. *Raising the Challenging Child: How to Minimize Meltdowns, Reduce Conflict, and Increase Cooperation.*

102

15-MINUTE FOCUS
Regulation and Co-Regulation: Accessible Neuroscience and
Connection Strategies that Bring Calm into the Classroom

Grand Rapids, Revell, A Division Of Baker Publishing Group, 2020.

13, 27, 34, 92   Hughes, Daniel A, and Jonathan F Baylin. *Brain-Based Parenting: The Neuroscience of Caregiving for Healthy Attachment.* New York, W.W. Norton & Co, 2012.

14, 77   Hughes, Daniel A. *Building the Bonds of Attachment: Awakening Love in Deeply Traumatized Children.* Lanham, Maryland, Rowman & Littlefield, 2018.

16, 17, 18, 19, 20, 33, 36, 37, 42, 49, 53   Place, Jodi. *Supporting Emotional Regulation in the Classroom (Quick Reference Guide).* ASCD, 27 May 2021.

21, 35   Harris, Nadine Burke. *The Deepest Well: Healing the Long-Term Effects of Childhood Adversity.* London, England, Bluebirds Books For Life, 2018.

22, 24, 25, 26, 40, 81   Beem, J. (2022, October 27). *The voice for traumatized children and families.* Attachment and Trauma Network. https://www.attachmenttraumanetwork.org/

23, 83   Purvis, Karyn B, et al. *The Connected Child: Bring Hope and Healing to Your Adoptive Family.* New York, Mcgraw-Hill, 2007.

28   Team, B. H. E. (2022, December 22). *How mirror neurons help you relate to others.* BetterHelp. https://www.betterhelp.com/advice/behavior/how-mirror-neurons-help-you-relate-to-others/

29, 31   "Neurotypical: All You Need to Know and More." *Neurotypical: All You Need to Know and More,* www.healthline.com/health/neurotypical.

30, 54, 55   Siegel, Daniel J, and Tina Payne Bryson. *The Whole-Brain Child: 12 Revolutionary Strategies to Nurture Your Child's Developing Mind.* New York, Bantam Books, 2012.

15-MINUTE FOCUS
Regulation and Co-Regulation: Accessible Neuroscience and
Connection Strategies that Bring Calm into the Classroom

103

32 Holly Van Gulden, and Charlotte Vick. *Learning the Dance of Attachment: An Adoptive Parent's Guide to Fostering Healthy Development.* Minneapolis, Minnesota, Holly Van Gulden, and Charlotte Vick, 2010.

38,45,66 "Center on the Developing Child at Harvard University." *Center on the Developing Child at Harvard University*, 2019, developingchild. harvard.edu/.

39,65 Brummer, J., & Thorsborne, M. (2021). *Building A Trauma-informed Restorative School: skills and approaches for improving culture and behavior.* Jessica Kingsley Publishers.

41 Hoffman, Kent. *Raising a Secure Child: How Circle of Security Parenting Can Help You Nurture Your Child's Attachment, Emotional Resilience, and Freedom to Explore.* New York, Guilford Press, 2017.

43, 44, 47, 71, 85, 86, 87, 88, 90, 94 Nagoski, Emily, and Amelia Nagoski. *Burnout: The Secret to Unlocking the Stress Cycle.* New York, Ballantine Books, 2020.

46, 52, 59, 80, 84, 98 Perry, Bruce. "ChildTrauma Academy." *Child Trauma Academy*, 2020, www.childtrauma.org/.

48 Daniels, Emily Read. *The Regulated Classroom: Bottom-up Trauma-Informed Teaching.* Here This Now, LLC., 11 Feb. 2020.

50 Felitti, Vincent J., et al. "Relationship of Childhood Abuse and Household Dysfunction to Many of the Leading Causes of Death in Adults: The Adverse Childhood Experiences (ACE) Study." *American Journal of Preventive Medicine*, vol. 56, no. 6, June 2019, pp. 774–786, 10.1016/j.amepre.2019.04.001.

56, 58, 62, 70, 73 Perez, K. (2021). Building NeuroResilience. ESSDACKOnline. https://online.essdack.org/p/neurores.

15-MINUTE FOCUS
Regulation and Co-Regulation: Accessible Neuroscience and
Connection Strategies that Bring Calm into the Classroom

63, 99, 101 Desautels, Lori L. *Connections over Compliance: Rewiring Our Perceptions of Discipline.* Deadwood, Oregon, Wyatt-Mackenzie Publishing, 2021.

74 Sporleder, J. (October 14, 2022) [Conference address] Compliance to Compassion Conference

75 Moffett, J. (October, 14. 2022) [Keynote address] Compliance to Compassion Conference

78 Baylin, Jonathan F, and Daniel A Hughes. *The Neurobiology of Attachment-Focused Therapy: Enhancing Connection and Trust in the Treatment of Children and Adolescents.* New York, W.W. Norton & Company, 2016.

79, 97, 100 Perry, B. D., & Winfrey, O. (2022). *What happened to you?: Conversations on trauma, resilience, and healing.* Bluebird.

82 Sinarski, Jessica. *Riley the Brave's Sensational Senses.* Jessica Kingsley Publishers, 10 Oct. 2022.

89, 91 Leaf Group. (n.d.). *What is community care and what are its health benefits? | Livestrong.* LIVESTRONG.COM. https://www.livestrong.com/article/13771535-self-care-vs-community-care/

93 Golding, Kim S, and Daniel A Hughes. *Creating Loving Attachments : Parenting with PACE to Nurture Confidence and Security in the Troubled Child.* London ; Philadelphia, Jessica Kingsley Publishers, 2012.

95 Carnegie Corporation of New York. (n.d.). *A playbook for effectively engaging families and schools: Family & Community engagement.* Carnegie Corporation of New York. https://www.carnegie.org/our-work/article/playbook-effectively-engaging-families-and-schools/

15-MINUTE FOCUS
Regulation and Co-Regulation: Accessible Neuroscience and
Connection Strategies that Bring Calm into the Classroom

105

Resources

1. Trauma-Informed and Attachment Focused Free Resources for Caregivers and Educators: www.attachmenttraumanetwork.org/

2. Trauma-Informed Podcast: https://anchor.fm/regulatedandrelational

3. Resilience Survey: https://originstraining.org/aces/resilience-survey/

4. Healing Mantras: https://community.thriveglobal.com/11-powerful-mantras-for-healing/

5. Journal Prompts: https://www.waterford.org/resources/journal-prompts-for-kids/

6. Fun Breathing for Kids: https://cosmickids.com/five-fun-breathing-exercises-for-kids/

DOWNLOADABLE RESOURCES

The resources in this book are available for you as a digital download!

Please visit **15minutefocusseries.com** and click this book cover on the page. Once you've clicked the book cover, a prompt will ask you for a code to unlock the activities.

Please enter code:

Regulation510

106

15-MINUTE FOCUS
Regulation and Co-Regulation: Accessible Neuroscience and
Connection Strategies that Bring Calm into the Classroom

Acknowledgments

To Julie Beem, my visionary leader.

To Dr. Melissa Sadin, my inspiration and mentor.

To Jodi Place, my cheerleader and wise colleague.

And to my family, my oxygen and complete joy.

15-MINUTE FOCUS
Regulation and Co-Regulation: Accessible Neuroscience and
Connection Strategies that Bring Calm into the Classroom

107

About the Author

GINGER HEALY, MSW, LCSW is a clinical social worker with almost 30 years of experience in the field of social work. Ginger has worked as a child abuse investigator, hospital social worker, and school therapist. She spent 15 years as the social service supervisor at an international adoption agency and was able to travel to provide support for orphanages all over the world. This job taught her so much about attachment and trauma needs in children. She currently works as the program director for the Attachment and Trauma Network where she co-anchors the podcast "Regulated & Relational" and speaks across the nation on trauma-informed schools, therapeutic parenting, and community engagement. She is married with four children who have been her greatest teachers about developmental trauma and special needs. She loves to travel and read.

108

15-MINUTE FOCUS
Regulation and Co-Regulation: Accessible Neuroscience and
Connection Strategies that Bring Calm into the Classroom

A Brief Look at Ginger's Workshop Sessions

Emotional Regulation and Co-Regulation for the Classroom

Ginger brings hope into classrooms by teaching the importance of educator regulation and co-regulation strategies. Ginger makes neuroscience accessible and shares the three steps of the regulation cycle that can bring calm and healing into the classroom. She demonstrates how regulation of the educator's nervous system is crucial in managing the behaviors and big feelings in the classroom while sharing easy-to-implement strategies that can work for any child. This session will empower educators to lower the stress levels of both students and themselves.

Trauma-Informed Education

Ginger discusses and explains trauma-sensitive schools - what they are and what the paradigm shift surrounding them looks like. She helps attendees understand the pervasiveness of trauma and its impact on student learning and teaches how to recognize the signs and respond with a trauma-sensitive approach to avoid re-traumatization. This session will provide participants with strategies to implement in the classroom that support students through safety, regulation, and connection.

Neuroplasticity: We Can Change Brains!

Ginger makes neuroscience fascinating and fun as she explores strategies that re-wire a child's brain from chaos to calm. Ginger gives an experiential lesson on the hand-brain model that empowers children to manage their feelings and behaviors, moving them out of shame and into post-traumatic growth. This session will introduce participants to brain basics that are essential to understanding in order to shape educator response to behaviors.

For the Givers: Preventing Burnout for Educators

What exactly is burnout? How do you know when you are approaching it, and can it be avoided? Ginger explores self-care and community care strategies while teaching how to complete the stress cycle. Ginger will teach research-based implementations that can be put into place immediately and will help educators start on the road to healing. This session is dedicated to "all the givers" who will walk away inspired and energized with a concrete plan to move forward.

Creating Calm Kits and Regulation Rooms

Ginger discusses the importance of "felt-safety" and creating safe spaces in the classroom and throughout the entire school building. Ginger will break down how to create a calm kit and regulation room and will also share dos and don'ts for each. Participants will walk away with a How-To formula, including a list of rules, a list of supplies, and a new lens of thinking when it comes to behavior management.

The Importance of Relationships: Connecting with Hard-to-Reach Students

Ginger discusses attachment- what it is, how it's developed, and why it's important for academic success. She explores buffer relationships and attunement to student needs. She digs into teacher triggers and how to look at behaviors that get under our skin. Ginger will offer strategies for removing barriers that block academic success and emotional healing. Participants will make a paradigm shift in understanding behaviors and be able to implement strategies to help children reach academic success and get on the path to healing adversities.

To learn more, visit ncyionline.org/speakers

15-MINUTE FOCUS
Regulation and Co-Regulation: Accessible Neuroscience and
Connection Strategies that Bring Calm into the Classroom

109

Look for these books in the series!

DIGITAL CITIZENSHIP
Supporting Youth Navigating Technology
in a Rapidly Changing World

Dr. Raychelle Cassada Lohmann and Dr. Angie Smith

GROWTH MINDSET, RESILIENCE, AND GRIT
Harnessing Internal Superpowers
for Student Success

Dr. Raychelle Cassada Lohmann

DIVERSITY, BIAS, AND PRIVILEGE
Addressing Racial Inequities to Create
Inclusive Learning Environments

Dr. Natalie Spencer Gwyn and Robert B. Jamison

ANGER, RAGE, AND AGGRESSION

Dr. Raychelle Cassada Lohmann

BEHAVIOR INTERVENTIONS
Strategies for Educators, Counselors,
and Parents

Amie Dean

BEHAVIOR INTERVENTIONS WORKBOOK
Your Roadmap for Creating a Positive
Classroom Community

Amie Dean

110

15-MINUTE FOCUS
Regulation and Co-Regulation: Accessible Neuroscience and
Connection Strategies that Bring Calm into the Classroom